P9-CQQ-847

THE WINTERTHUR GARDEN

Henry Francis du Pont's Romance with the Land

DENISE MAGNANI

with

WILLIAM H. FREDERICK, JR.

JACQUELINE HINSLEY

ROBERT F. TRENT

PAUL HENSLEY

THOMAS BUCHTER

Research Assistance by RUTH N. JOYCE

New Photography by

CAROL BETSCH

Harry N. Abrams, Inc., Publishers
in association with
The Henry Francis du Pont Winterthur Museum, Inc.

For everyone
who has "loved and taken care of"
the Winterthur garden

Page 1: Climbing roses in the Sycamore Area bloom throughout the summer.
Pages 2–3: Flowering dogwood, azaleas, and Spanish bluebells are visible from the Blue Room.
Pages 4–5: The Winterthur landscape at dawn.
Pages 6–7: Italian windflowers in Azalea Woods.
Inset page 6: Dexter hybrid rhododendron 'Frances Shannon Racoff.'

For Harry N. Abrams, Inc.:
PROJECT MANAGER: *Mark D. Greenberg*
EDITOR: *Jennifer Stockman*
DESIGNER: *Maria Learmonth Miller*

For Winterthur:
EDITOR: *Onie Rollins*
COPY EDITOR: *Teresa A. Vivolo*

Excerpt from "Notes Toward a Supreme Fiction" from Collected Poems *by Wallace Stevens.*
Copyright 1942 by Wallace Stevens.
Reprinted by permission of Alfred A. Knopf, Inc. and Faber and Faber Limited

LIBRARY OF CONGRESS CATALOGING-IN-PUBLICATION DATA
The Winterthur garden : Henry Francis du Pont's romance with the land / essays
by Denise Magnani ... [et al.] ; photography by Carol Betsch ; research assistance by Ruth N. Joyce.
p. cm.
Includes bibliographical references and index.
ISBN 0–8109–3779–4
1. *Henry Francis du Pont Winterthur Museum Gardens (Del.)—History.*
2. *Henry Francis du Pont Winterthur Museum—History.*
3. *Du Pont, Henry Francis, 1880–1969—Homes and haunts—Delaware.*
I. *Magnani, Denise.* II. *Henry Francis du Pont Winterthur Museum.*
SB466.U7H467 1995
712'.5'097511—dc20   94–14976
                                                CIP

Copyright © 1995 The Henry Francis du Pont Winterthur Museum, Inc.
Carol Betsch photographs copyright © 1995 Carol Betsch

Published in 1995 by Harry N. Abrams, Incorporated, New York
A Times Mirror Company
All rights reserved. No part of the contents of this book may be reproduced
without the written permission of the publisher

Printed and bound in Japan

Contents

I was born at Winterthur,
and I have always loved everything connected with it.

HENRY FRANCIS DU PONT 1952

DIRECTOR'S FOREWORD

Dwight P. Lanmon

In 1951 Henry Francis du Pont opened his home to the public. Over the ensuing years, Winterthur has taken its place at the forefront of museums devoted to American decorative arts. I first came here in 1966 as a graduate student in the Winterthur Program in Early American Culture. When I returned in 1992 to assume the responsibilities of director, it was with great enthusiasm and anticipation. I felt as if I were coming home.

The institution has grown and changed with time. Many new tours, seminars, workshops, trips, children's activities, and events expand upon the basic guided tours of period rooms that have been the mainstay of our programming since 1951. The Galleries, a beautiful building opened in 1992, displays objects individually and offers visitors the opportunity to view them at their own pace. Of the changes I found, however, none surprised me more than the activity in the garden.

Among the most vivid memories of my student days are moments that friends and I shared in the garden. In late January we eagerly searched for the first harbingers of spring—drifts of snowdrops blooming on the March Bank. It was also a treat to make soup from watercress gathered at the little stream in the Quarry Garden.

During my first speech to the staff as director, I pointed out how different, how stark and uninviting the museum might seem were it not surrounded by more than 900 acres of rolling hills, clear streams, open meadows, and stands of trees. I was a bit disconcerted to find that the garden staff did not fully appreciate my comments. Not that they disagreed; they were well aware of the "peace and great calm," as H. F. du Pont himself had put it, of the Winterthur landscape. They wanted me, however, to say more, to go further. They wanted me to become the garden's champion.

On several memorable occasions, Thomas Buchter, deputy director of the newly created Garden Department, literally took me on a journey of discovery, sometimes to corners of the estate that I had never visited. During those trips Thomas discoursed on the artistic integrity of the garden, on the difficulties inherent in attempting to restore du Pont's design intent, and on the necessity of preserving the historic agricultural landscape. Denise

Fireflies by the old gate on Gate House Road.

Magnani also helped expand my garden perspective. It was she who had gathered together the select group of authors who were putting the finishing touches on a biography of the garden, defining H. F. du Pont as the creator of a masterpiece of twentieth-century American naturalism.

Of course, they won me over. I now speak as passionately as anyone about the value and meaning of the garden. I am particularly fascinated by du Pont's integration of the elements of his composition. With a master designer's sleight of hand, he ensured that every visitor to his museum would also experience the garden. What else is the half-mile entry drive but a journey away from the cares of the world and into nature's domain? When he commissioned the Visitor Pavilion in 1960 he instructed the architects, his cousins Samuel and Victorine du Pont Homsey, to "make it look as if it isn't there." Their award-winning building seems to be an organic part of the landscape.

H. F. du Pont also had a good understanding of *human* nature. He worked diligently to "get the thing going" (the museum, garden, library, and graduate programs) but admitted that "it is useless to lay down too many rules" for the future directors and caretakers of Winterthur. We, therefore, have the responsibility and the freedom to bring his vision of the past into a vital future.

The heart of our mission has always been the conservation of the collection of American decorative arts. We now realize that both the rural and designed landscapes are as precious—and have become as rare—as any object in the museum. It will be an important task of my administration to protect this great resource and make the Winterthur landscape even more accessible to our public. The Winterthur garden is more than a beautiful setting; it is one of our crown jewels.

Staircase from the East Terrace to the Reflecting Pool in early May. The azaleas are R. *'Coral Bells' and lavender 'Winterthur.' The chartreuse blossoms are* Viburnum macrocephalum *'Sterile,' and the small trees are white flowering dogwood and purple-leaf filbert.*

PREFACE

Denise Magnani

It was one of those radiant days in June when everyone is ineluctably drawn outdoors. As curator and director of landscape in the Garden Department at Winterthur, my job description provided a built-in excuse to flee the confines of the office: I had to see how the garden was growing.

I hopped in a golf cart (our game is gardening, but we keep a few carts on hand just for such curatorial emergencies), headed down Farm Hill Road, turned left on Old Gate House Road, which becomes Museum Road at the base of the hill, and drove into the garden in search of the season's last Dexter hybrid rhododendron blossoms.

As is perhaps evident, much of Winterthur's social and natural history is quite literally written on the land in the form of road signs and building names. The Meadow Parking Area, Buzzard Lane, and Duck Pond are all apt descriptors. Saw Mill Road attests to Winterthur's past as a nearly self-sufficient country estate at the turn of the century. Clenny Run, Chandler Farm, and Armor Woods are all reminders of families connected with the original Winterthur farmland.

The link between Winterthur's agrarian past and its present as a noted cultural institution is Henry Francis du Pont (1880–1969), the last private owner of the property and creator of the garden that is a masterpiece of twentieth-century naturalism, the renowned museum of American decorative arts, and the library, a research center for the interdisciplinary study of American art, material culture, and history. Winterthur was his life's work, yet he was always at pains to point out that Winterthur had been "loved and taken care of for three generations" of his family.

The seeds of the Winterthur garden were sown during Harry's childhood. He and his sister, Louise, grew up surrounded by the beauty of Winterthur and encouraged by attentive parents who taught them to appreciate nature. As a young man, Harry studied at Bussey Institution, Harvard's college of practical agriculture and horticulture, at the dawn of an era often described as "the golden age of American horticulture." There he was exposed to the most exciting design ideas of his time and formed a lasting friendship with Marian

Come into the garden. In 1928 Marian Coffin designed the circular Box Scroll Garden, here enhanced with tulips, to help link the house and garden.

Overleaf: Queen Anne's lace has transformed a field into a wildflower garden. H. F. du Pont said of the agricultural landscape, "No amount of landscaping or planting can improve it."

Coffin, one of the first American women to become a landscape architect. During the next sixty years of gardening at Winterthur, Harry mastered the gentle art of designing with nature.

Harry worked naturalistically, his methods based not only on scientific knowledge but also on what he learned as a lifelong observer of the world around him. Like many other modern artists, he broke with the formal traditions of the past in seeking a new vocabulary to express his vision. So skillfully did he harmonize his garden with the agricultural landscape, echo the colors of woodland and meadow flowers, and amplify natural cycles and succession of bloom that many visitors attribute the garden's informal beauty to chance, little more than a series of happy coincidences. Nothing could be further from the truth. Few plots of land in North America have received more thoughtful, continuous stewardship and experimentation than the roughly 200 acres that comprise the Winterthur garden.

The story of the garden, however, is not Harry's story alone. It cannot be told without mention of the "three generations" of du Ponts and everyone else who lived and worked at Winterthur. To recount such an epic, we enlisted the aid of landscape architect William H. Frederick, Jr., as well as specialists from different departments within Winterthur and neighboring institutions.

As a young man, Bill Frederick came to know H. F. du Pont as a mature garden artist. Frederick's chapter is a personal tribute to a mentor and a valuable professional assessment of du Pont's contribution to the American garden.

Jacqueline Hinsley was research associate at Hagley Museum and Library (the premier repository for du Pont corporate and family papers) for many years. She delves into the history of the du Ponts, with a particular interest in the philosophical traditions that nurtured their Brandywine Valley garden legacy: Eleutherian Mills (Hagley), Longwood Gardens, Nemours, and Winterthur.

Robert F. Trent, curator and in charge of furniture at Winterthur, has written extensively on seventeenth-century American furniture. He welcomed the opportunity to go "outside" his field and explore the house and garden relationship that he first noticed more than twenty years ago as a student in the Winterthur Program in Early American Culture.

Paul Hensley, now associate director of development, was Winterthur archivist for eight years. He expertly traces the history of the scientifically run dairy operation that was an integral part of daily life on the estate up to recent times.

Thomas Buchter is the first deputy director of the Garden Department, which was formed by the Winterthur Board of Trustees in 1988 to manage the garden professionally and bring it into a glorious second century. Buchter's essay on restoring a great American garden is a fitting epilogue to an inspirational tale.

"Postscripts" were assembled by Ruth N. Joyce, researcher for this book. Letters she retrieved from the archives provide an immediacy and authenticity that no author could duplicate.

Landscape photographer Carol Betsch of Ithaca, New York, completed the majority of the new color photography between 1990 and 1993. Her work captures the power and fragility of the garden treasure that is in our safekeeping.

We knew from the beginning that we were writing a love story, incorporating many of love's aspects: from a family's reverence for the land to a little boy's wonder at the real world; from a youthful infatuation with plants to a mature commitment to a painstaking design process. H. F. du Pont never wore his heart on his sleeve, but he expressed his feelings for nature in his joyful, lyrical, romantic garden. Harry put his heart into the garden, and then he gave it away.

THE ARTIST IN HIS GARDEN

William H. Frederick, Jr.

There ought to be gardens for all the months of the year, in
which, severally, things of beauty may be then in season.
SIR FRANCIS BACON, ON GARDENS 1625

I am interested in getting a successive bloom in the spring.
H. F. DU PONT 1962

There is no doubt in my mind that the Winterthur garden is one of the great gardens of
the world. What circumstances brought this garden into existence?

One has to think in terms of chance, I believe. Just as a seed dropped in a site ideal
for it to flourish does exactly that, Henry Francis du Pont's artistic talents were fortunate
enough to connect with a landscape whose beauty he could uniquely maximize.

The acreage involved is without question rare and wonderful. The landforms have
great sculptural beauty. The native vegetation and agricultural scene with which du Pont
started are unequaled. Horticulturally the soil is excellent, and the site is neither unusually
windy nor a frost pocket. H. F. du Pont's love of this site amounted to a passion.

His equally passionate interest in ornamental plants started early, preceding his interest
in American decorative arts, and was encouraged by a consistent curiosity and drive to learn
more. Du Pont's determination to join these two passions—his love of the site and the plants
—in an aesthetically successful manner is the key, I believe, to this garden's unique success.

The garden is amazing in its complexity and, although seamlessly whole, can best be
understood as a series of seasonal garden experiences joined by circulatory paths (page 20).
In this sense it is an American version of a Japanese stroll garden. Areas are further joined by
a superbly calculated choreography as declining bloom in one area overlaps the beginning of
plant interest in another. This attribute of flowing choreography was essential to the way

*Gardeners must not be overeager
in removing the fallen leaves
of our native sour gum on Oak
Hill. Nyssa sylvatica, whose
apt Latin name translates as
"water sprite of the woodlands,"
is the first tree to color in late
September. When its leaves
drift among the translucent
colchicum chalices, we drink
a toast to H. F. du Pont, who
once again arranged his old
standby, lavender and scarlet,
to perform on cue.*

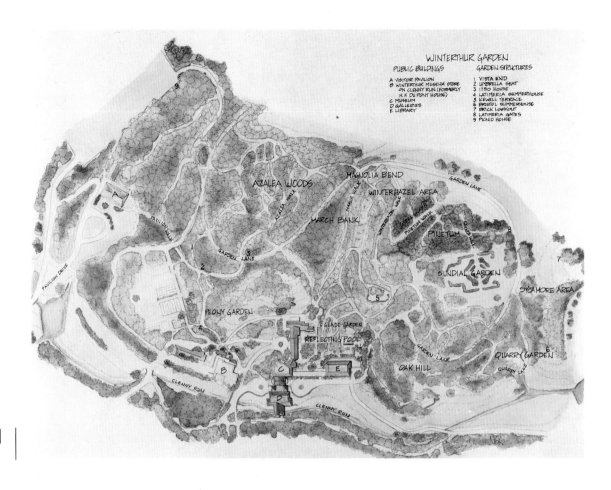

Winterthur Garden map.

du Pont used the garden. His life was highly social; barely a week passed without visitors from out of town. A changing exhibition perfectly suited the frequent forays into the garden that provided him and his guests with enormous pleasure. During the months that H. F. du Pont lived at Winterthur there were no aesthetic vacuums.

July and August were frequently the months when, prior to his marriage, H. F. du Pont traveled in Europe visiting and studying gardens. After their marriage in 1916, he and Mrs. du Pont spent summers at Chestertown House, their home on Long Island. Activity in the garden at Winterthur was minimal while they were not in residence there. A bit more horticultural display resumed in autumn, when the du Ponts returned. Seasonal interest came then from the incomparable color of foliage in the woodlands and, until the herbaceous gardens were removed in 1957, from the color of these borders. The du Ponts spent February and most of March in Boca Grande, Florida, returning to Winterthur by

Easter. The spring display was just heating up and breaking forth in all its glory by the time they arrived. Activity during the spring months predominated when the du Ponts' multiresidence life was centered at Winterthur and H. F. du Pont had the most extensive and quickly changing palette of plants with which to work. During this season the challenge was greatest, the success most noteworthy.

Du Pont's appetite for knowledge about plants and garden design was avid. Aside from the time he spent studying at Bussey Institution in Massachusetts, he was largely self-taught. All ornamental plants interested him, but learning and collecting focused around several themes. Whenever he became enthusiastic about a particular plant, say, a viburnum, he would want to learn about all others in that genus. Also, his interest in a specific genus, such as iris, would whet his appetite for extending its principal blooming season. Likewise, if he became interested in composing a picture during a certain season of the year, he would want to know about other plants that bloomed at the same time.

It was inevitable that this interest would bring him into contact with the complete roster of plantspersons of his day, particularly plant breeders such as David Leach, Henry Skinner, Charles O. Dexter, and A. Percy Saunders. New plants from this community flowed constantly to Winterthur. In some instances H. F. du Pont placed the plants directly into the garden in predesignated spots. More often than not he put them in the nursery, where their performance, color, and habit could be observed before they were incorporated as part of a garden scheme. He would eventually reject some and use others. It is estimated that du Pont tested at least five plants for every one he finally chose.

It is an immense tribute to this man that although he was an avid plant enthusiast carrying the torch for all that was new and best for American gardens, no part of the Winterthur garden has the feel of a collection. Du Pont had the ability and persistence to deal with myriad details while keeping in mind a larger, higher priority—the total garden experience in terms of both color and choreography.

The soul-satisfying color combinations and choreography were not usually the result of a single inspiration at a single moment. A long-term interest and commitment involved refinements over a period of time. This process is something that most mature gardeners are prepared to carry out, and H. F. du Pont serves as a great example to those who are just beginning.

MARCH BANK

The part of the garden to bloom earliest is the March Bank. Except for woodland trees, this show is cast almost entirely with herbaceous plants and strongly emphasizes diminutive

A few of the famous horticulturists who supplied plants to H. F. du Pont:

Clement G. Bowers, *rhododendrons*
G. Percy Brown, *iris*
W. B. Clarke, *chaenomeles*
Charles O. Dexter, *rhododendrons*
H. Lincoln Foster, Primula abschasica
Joseph B. Gable, *rhododendrons and azaleas*
William Gratwick, *peonies*
Henry Hohman, *syringa, etc.*
David Leach, *native azaleas*
G. G. Nearing, Ilex pernyi, *rhododendrons, azaleas*
Carl Purdy, *erythroniums, hellebores, etc.*
Charles S. Sargent, *many species*
A. Percy Saunders, *peonies*
Silvia Saunders, *peonies*
Arthur H. Scott, *iris*
Henry Skinner, *native azaleas*
Arlow B. Stout, *hemerocallis*
Patrick Synge, *narcissus*
Thomas Wheeldon, *rhododendrons*
Ellen Willmott, *perennials*
John C. Wister, *iris*

Spring snowflake and Amur adonis bloom together in late winter on the March Bank. They were planted there about 1910. In 1962 H. F. du Pont admitted to an interviewer, "For years I kept records of when the first flowers came out, and I still do as a matter of fact."

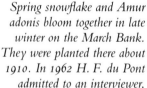

Opposite: One of H. F. du Pont's favorite color combinations was lavender and yellow. This little Iris reticulata *cultivar displays both colors in each blossom. A drift of them grows on the Quarry Garden bank, just below eye level, where the diminutive (3–4") plants can best be appreciated.*

spring bulbs, creating a Botticellian effect under the leafless trees in the late winter and early spring months.

The season of interest is long and is the best example in one area of the garden of a flowing succession of bloom. The remarkable flexibility of this complex sequencing during capricious weather that is never the same for two consecutive years is a compliment to both the plants involved and the genius of du Pont's arrangement. The cast is enormous. Late February and early March find white snowdrops (*Galanthus*, in variety) running through the woods and joined on the famous bank by two yellow-flowered members of the buttercup family: winter aconite (*Eranthis hyemalis*), which is quite short, and the rarer nonbulbous *Adonis amurensis*, which is taller and has fernlike foliage. At the same time, the spring snowflake (*Leucojum vernum*) presents its green-tipped, fresh white bells (this page). These are joined in early March by the exquisite lavender blossoms of *Crocus tomasinianus*, which on cloudy days close and show off their beautiful silver exteriors. During March the cast gradually changes to sheets of blue glory-of-the-snow (*Chionodoxa luciliae*) and *Scilla sibirica*, with yellow blossoms on the cornelian-cherry (*Cornus mas*), a small tree. Early in the season the sequence of bloom may be interrupted by snow and ice, but as soon as the temperature rises, the cavalcade rolls on. After the bleakness of winter this symphony of white, yellow, and blue lifts spirits and provides assurance that spring really will come (opposite).

Native wildflowers, including the true blue Brandywine bluebells (*Mertensia virginica*), carry through May. A pause comes in early June as tree leaves become full blown. In late June and early July the lower banks and valley floor are carpeted with bold fern massings and showy blossoms on shade-tolerant perennials: roving bellflower (*Campanula rapunculoides*), white snakeroot (*Cimicifuga racemosa*), tall meadow-rue (*Thalictrum polygamum*), and blue plantainlily (*Hosta ventricosa*).

WINTERHAZEL WALK

The second major event in the garden occurs on the Winterhazel Walk. The color display, of shorter duration than the March Bank extravaganza, reaches a breathtakingly beautiful peak in early April. Two shrubs are the major actors: several species of winterhazel (*Corylopsis*), which hangs bells of soft greenish yellow along its branches, and Korean rhododendron (*Rhododendron mucronulatum*), with its leafless branches covered with lavender

blossoms of a shade that makes the blue of the spring sky even richer (opposite). This area is undoubtedly one of H. F. du Pont's major aesthetic achievements. The color combination is thoroughly exciting and satisfying—a cool yellow contrasted with a warm lavender. Other shrubs are used for reinforcement, particularly *Prinsepia sinensis*, with bright green, small, young leaves that appear just as the winterhazel blossoms open.

Below this planting a rich ground cover of herbaceous beauty further enriches the scene. Among the players are large drifts of selected forms of *Helleborus orientalis* (page 28, inset), such as 'Atrorubens' and 'Mons Prosperi Perthuis,' with emphasis on wine, pink, and chartreuse blossoms; *Corydalis bulbosa*, with blossoms a shade lighter than the Korean rhododendron blossoms; and *Primula abschasica* and *Lathyrus vernus*, appearing late in April with flowers nearly the color of the rhododendron.

GREENSWARD

Left open as a major vista from the house and parallel in timing and location with the Winterhazel Walk is the Greensward, which rises to meet two specimen Sargent cherries (*Prunus sargentii*). The theme is pink, and we feel the excitement H. F. du Pont must have experienced in bringing together this rich palette. There are pink forms of Korean rhododendron, including 'Cornell Pink'; several good selections and hybrids of fragrant viburnum (*Viburnum farreri*), including 'Candidissimum'; and both shrub cherries, such as *Prunus tomentosa* and the tree form *Prunus* 'Accolade,' which was H. F. du Pont's favorite (page 26). This planting is largely on the west side of the Greensward; the darkness of the Pinetum dominates on the east side. The bright green of the lawn in April links the two and provides the perfect unifier for the large palette of plants in the pink planting. A typical H. F. du Pont touch simultaneously knocks us off balance and brings a sense of order to all this pink diversity: a handsome Japanese white pine (*Pinus parviflora* 'Glauca') is about halfway along the rich pink assemblage, towering above a clump of *Narcissus* 'Hunter's Moon,' whose blossoms are a most wondrous soft greenish yellow, a hue that causes all the pinks to sing.

QUINCE WALK

Of equally short duration, approximately two weeks in late April, is the flowering season of the Quince Walk (page 27). As a color tour de force it is certainly one of the richest in the garden because so many hues have been used together successfully. We can barely resist singing for joy as we come upon it. The basic ingredient is a large number of flowering quince cultivars, most of which H. F. du Pont received from the breeder, W. B. Clarke, in

The Winterhazel Walk comes into full bloom before most deciduous spring leaves have begun to unfold. Without the dampening aspect of green interspersed throughout the planting, the contrasting color scheme of pale yellow winterhazel and rosy lavender Korean rhododendron, carried out in all of the herbaceous ground covers, is even more intense and represents a simple idea taken to its logical artistic conclusion. The area was thirty-five years in the making, but the great 2½- to 3-week show each year has been worth the wait.

⬧

Loveliest of trees, the cherries now play their cameo role. A magnificent pair of Sargent cherries, more than seventy-five years old, are pink in bud, nearly white in flower. Across Garden Lane, Prunus 'Accolade' has yet to open its frilly, palest pink blossoms. The fragrant viburnums and pink forms of Rhododendron mucronulatum *join the ensemble, a show-stopper against the dramatic April sky.*

California. The range is immense: light red, blood red, brick, dark red with yellow center, orange, salmon, carmine, light pink, white, and a pink that is somewhere between salmon and yellow. Intermixed are early viburnums such as *V. carlesii*. The immediate background is the green shades of the Pinetum; to the south and west are crabapples and early lavender rhododendron cultivars.

Among this latter group is a combination I try to see in bloom every year: an ancient Parkman crabapple (*Malus halliana* 'Parkmannii') that has large blossoms presented pendulously on the longest stems of any crabapple I know. These are of an unusual true carmine pink and are held elegantly on the branches, some of which hang to the grass below where the bulbous spring starflower (*Ipheion uniflorum*) from Argentina has been naturalized and displays its gray-blue flowers.

Part of the Quince Walk planting graces the sides of a path that passes through the dark Pinetum. It is here that *Spiraea arguta*, with its graceful habit and delicate white blossoms, has been used to push the color of the flowering quince. The real peak of achievement comes on the hillside below, where the chartreuse flower buds of *Viburnum macrocephalum forma macrocephalum* make the great cornucopia of quince colors work so well.

AZALEA WOODS

Justly famous, Azalea Woods peaks in the first half of May; however, early spring bulbs flower in March. *Rhododendron fargesii*; Italian windflower (*Anemone apennina*); various primulas, such as *Primula elatior, P. veris*, and *P. vulgaris*; and the exquisite white of *Trillium grandiflorum* follow in close sequence. Likewise, the season extends to the middle of June with evergreen rhododendron hybrids, wildflowers in late May, and Martagon lily hybrids in early June. The great accomplishment is the magnificent orchestration of early May, when the color harmonies of the azaleas are at their peak and the herbaceous ground plants are full of splendor.

A triangular open space has been left in the center of Azalea Woods. It is filled with an overwhelming assortment of woodland charmers, including white (*Trillium grandiflorum*) and yellow (*T. sessile* 'Luteum') trillium, Brandywine bluebells (*Mertensia virginica*), and yellow bellwort (*Uvularia grandiflora*). Around this space the great color spectacle of the azaleas moves out in all directions above a carpet of blue-flowered scilla (*Endymion hispanicus*) (page 28). Shades of pink prevail, with white, deeper pink, and lavender also participating. We encounter a variety of courageous and successful twists as we stroll the paths. Only when we move to the highest elevation in the area and look down on the predominantly pink color scheme do we then realize that H. F. du Pont has highlighted the pink with a little orange (page 29, inset). In another area where some lavender has been used with the pink, one or two plants of shocking cherry red have been included (page 29). Du Pont's friend Silvia Saunders (daughter of peony hybridizer A. Percy Saunders) admired the vitality of the combination and asked him what made him decide to use those few discordant plants. He replied that they were meant to "chic it up." They do.

One large grouping of Kurume azaleas has been kept separate from Azalea Woods in a stretch of woodland at the intersection of Quarry and Garden lanes. Its deep pink shades are accompanied by no other color than green—that is, the new green of fully unfolded tree leaves. This simplicity provides a brilliant contrast to the complex color design of Azalea Woods and a most satisfying conclusion to the azalea season.

H. F. du Pont had a one-word answer to the question of how to turn a botanical collection into a garden: "Quince." In the 1930s he created a promenade of flowering quince cultivars beneath the towering evergreens of his father's Pinetum. In mid to late April, the brilliant quince blossoms illuminate the somber conifers.

Page 28: Sometimes a bluebell is white. Endymion hispanicus, the Spanish bluebell, has a white form, seen here scattered through the more common blues. Completing the bouquet are great white trilliums and azalea 'Snow' in bud.

*Page 28, inset: The Lenten rose (*Helleborus orientalis)* is one of the speckled, stippled, "dappled things" that Gerard Manley Hopkins celebrates in "Pied Beauty." The petals are cream sprinkled with chartreuse or mauve freckled with maroon.*

Page 29: The upright, cherry red azalea is 'Arnoldiana.' The mounded lavenders are known simply as "Kurume #4" and "#5." H. F. du Pont loved the synergistic effect these colors had on each other and found many opportunities to combine shades and tints of lavender and red throughout the Winterthur Garden.

Page 29, inset: In this long view, we can appreciate the separation of "near discords" in Azalea Woods. Marian Coffin used the phrase to describe some of the more daring and unusual color combinations her friend Harry created at Winterthur.

QUARRY GARDEN

The Quarry Garden, which reaches its peak in late May/early June, is quite different from Azalea Woods. Whereas Azalea Woods involves mounded shrubs so saturated with color that no foliage is visible, the Quarry Garden specialty is Asiatic (not Japanese) candelabra primroses that have several whorls of blossoms on each stem and, in mass, provide a light and airy effect with plenty of foliage visible. The color range is orange, pink, lavender, and soft yellow used in rich flowing masses (pages 32–33). In this case the special touch that H. F. du Pont used to give the color scheme a particular liveliness was a hybrid primula whose blossoms were tangerine. This plant was not reliably hardy. It would "go out" in cold winters. Undaunted, du Pont had his gardeners keep a few plants in protected frames and would pop them in the quarry bog as highlights were needed.

Minor players in the Quarry Garden area provide a less intense but sustained blossom interest from March to late May. One plant deserves specific mention both because it is another primula, *P. denticulata*, and because its form, a ball of flowers on a stick, and color, lavender, occur in April. These lavender varieties combine with the yellow of cornelian-cherry (*Cornus mas*), Japanese cornelian-cherry (*C. officinalis*), *Corydalis cheilanthifolia*, narcissus, and *Mahonia bealei*; the white of Japanese-andromeda (*Pieris japonica*); and the blue of Siberian scilla (*Scilla siberica*) and glory-of-the-snow (*Chionodoxa luciliae*) to provide a perfect appetizer for the pièce de résistance when the candelabra primroses are in full bloom.

PEONY GARDEN

The Peony Garden, on the walk west of the museum, has been planted with both woody and herbaceous peonies. A celebration of full-blown spring, it reaches its peak in late May but has a supporting cast of characters on both ends of the season. It is situated on a slope where grades have been cleverly handled. A pathway of alternating steps and ramps winds uphill to a small latticework arch, an architectural feature marking the vista's end. Because of the changes in grade and the skillful terracing, a series of intimate experiences enables the viewer to appreciate blossoms for their individual beauty. In the background are magnificent old blue-green false-cypress (*Chamaecyparis pisifera* 'Squarosa'), and pink weigela and beauty-bush (*Kolkwitzia amabilis*), pink and white (*Rhododendron mucronatum* 'Magnifica') and lavender (*R. mucronatum* 'Winterthur') azalea blossoms. Overhead, late in the peony season, are the pendulous white blossoms of the fragrant epaulette tree (*Pterostyrax hispida*).

The peonies themselves are a horticultural treasure comprising the best of the yellow, bronze, peach, and maroon Saunders tree peonies and an unparalleled planting of white, pink, and red herbaceous varieties selected with particular attention to flower form. *Cytisus praecox* 'Luteus,' with its soft yellow flowers, has been used to echo the yellow tree peonies' color in another texture. Two iris provide engaging detail along the steps: *I.* 'D. K. Williamson' and *I. graminea*, known as the plum tart iris because its blossoms bear that fragrance.

OAK HILL

A planting of particular interest in September, October, and November, started late in H. F. du Pont's life, is located on the east-facing edge of Oak Hill high above Clenny Run, where we have an impressive view of the lower ponds. A sour gum (*Nyssa sylvatica*) and several of the now-removed horizontally branched *Idesia polycarpa*, hung with panicles of showy red berries, once structured downhill views to the stream and the pond. The gum continues today to put on its show of crimson foliage just as the grassy bank beneath it bursts into a glory of lavender blossoms from the bulbous colchicum that have hidden, leafless, all summer (page 18).

Uphill to the west is a planting of shrubs with colorful fruit. The irregular spiky form of hardy-orange (*Poncirus trifoliata*) sports small, yellow lemons. Pendulous branches of tea viburnum (*V. setigerum*) are hung with orange-red berries. The lower-growing beautyberry (*Callicarpa dichotoma*) is smothered in clusters of purple fruit. The grass below this grouping sparkles in late September with the cheerful, yellow, crocuslike blossoms of so-called fall-daffodil (*Sternbergia lutea*).

CANONS OF DESIGN

If we are to learn about design from this garden, it is important to understand the guidelines to which H. F. du Pont adhered. From witnesses, correspondence, written notes, and orders for plants, we know a great deal about the process by which he achieved his results; yet, nowhere does he actually spell out any principles of design. Because I have loved and worked with similar landforms for forty-two years and because I share du Pont's passions for both the great cornucopia of plants available for our gardens and the potential of color and choreography as design tools, it has been natural for me to make the following subjective deductions.

1. *Respect the site; do not impose your will on it.* Du Pont deeply loved the native woodlands and agricultural scene. He capitalized on what was there rather than making major changes.

2. *Incorporate the garden into the existing landscape. The garden is not a separate entity.* Du Pont created vistas from the house and garden to the agricultural and woodland scenes, allowed the existing landscape to flow into the garden, and maintained open spaces in the garden that echo open spaces in the agricultural landscape.

 Architect Louis Kahn advised
his students to ask a building
what it "wants to be." The
Quarry Garden apparently
wanted to be a place where the
science of horticulture and the
art of gardening exuberantly
coalesced. The candelabra
primroses in the quarry bog are
P. x bullesiana in mixed colors;
the yellow are P. bulleyana;
leucothoë, in crevices, blooms
white bells; the variegated iris
is a cultivar of I. laevigata.
The mountain-laurel blossoms
are palest pink, a color that
gentles the delirious swath cut
through the rock by the primroses
in June.

33

3.   *Contrast richly, heavily planted areas with open space.* With this technique, du Pont gave the viewer's eye a restful change of pace between intensive experiences.

4.   *The garden is a social experience. It should be easily accessible and tempting to visitors on foot.* Du Pont made every effort to draw visitors farther and farther into the depths of the garden.

5.   *The style of planting design should be largely naturalistic—free flowing as in nature— except where strong rectilinear Renaissance design serves a special purpose.* The most obvious examples of the latter are in areas associated with the architecture of the house, such as the Reflecting Pool garden. Du Pont applied this principle to the Sundial Garden as well, which is situated at a point farthest from the house and roughly halfway in the circulatory path through the garden areas. This garden area serves the useful purpose of being an anchor of psychological security in what might otherwise appear to be an expanse of amorphous naturalism.

6.   *The driving force in the development of the garden should be colorful horticultural displays of hardy woody and herbaceous plants rather than sculpture, water displays, or other architectural elements.* Du Pont was a plant lover and took great interest in the enormous cornucopia of garden plants available and becoming available, including natives, alien introductions, and those newly created by plant breeders.

7.   *Develop a theme for each area of the garden and build the planting design of the area to enhance that theme.* Du Pont based themes sometimes on a particular genus, sometimes on a specific season of bloom, and sometimes on color. Azaleas, quince, peonies, and primroses provide examples of a genus used as a theme. Oak Hill, the March Bank, the Sundial Garden, and the Sycamore Area have seasonal themes. The Winterhazel Walk and the Greensward follow color themes. In each case, once H. F. du Pont chose a theme, he was highly disciplined in sticking to it and not cluttering the picture with unrelated plants or ideas.

8.   *Base site selection of each area on the requirements of the plants involved.* This often happened by trial—the test plantings of azaleas in the portion of the woodland opened up by the chestnut blight is a case in point—or serendipity. An example of the latter is the *Anemone apennina*, which was originally heavily planted on the March Bank and failed to thrive there; it subsequently appeared in Azalea Woods, where the plants were allowed room to spread and put on a breathtaking display.

9.   *After selecting a site and theme plants, add other plants that bloom at the same time to strengthen the feature; also add a few plants that bloom earlier and later where it seems appropriate to choreograph a modulated entrance and exit.* Winterhazel (*Corylopsis* in variety) and Korean rhododendron (*Rhododendron mucronulatum*) are the principal performers on the Winterhazel

Walk. H. F. du Pont added *Helleborus foetidus* and green shades of *H. orientalis* to pick up the green in the green-yellow winterhazel blossoms. He also added pink and maroon shades of *H. orientalis*, the lavender *Corydalis bulbosa* and *Lathyrus vernus,* and the mauve-flowered *Primula abschasica* to pick up the warm lavender of the Korean rhododendron. The main season of bloom on the Greensward centers around the pink *R. mucronulatum* 'Cornell Pink.' The picture starts unfolding, however, a week or two earlier with forms of *Viburnum farreri* and continues later with the pink of royal azalea (*R. schlippenbachii*) and *R.* 'Miss Susie.'

10.   *Plants, especially woody plants, should be spaced so that they are uncrowded and can show off their natural form.* This is clearly exemplified by several rearrangements that du Pont made. In the case of azaleas in Azalea Woods and quince on the Quince Walk, crowded, mature plants were dug up and replanted farther apart so the natural form of each plant would be visible in the years to come.

11.   *Plant as though making broad, bold brush strokes of single colors on a canvas.* Du Pont used large numbers of a single plant for the major colors in each composition. Snowdrops (*Galanthus*), *Crocus tomasinianus*, and *Chionodoxa lucilliae* are used by the thousands on the March Bank. Pink pearl azaleas (*Rhododendron* [Kurume] 'Pink Pearl') number in excess of fifty in Azalea Woods. Du Pont's color and textural combinations were successful because of this courageous approach.

12.   *In each color scheme look for the one small touch that can be added to enliven the picture.* This often involved du Pont's adding a few plants of an unexpected, even nonharmonious hue. Examples include the orange azaleas in the basically pink Azalea Woods, chartreuse *Viburnum* with *Chaenomeles* on the Quince Walk, and tangerine *Primula* in the Quarry Garden.

Although H. F. du Pont had studied the naturalistic gardens of Gertrude Jekyll, William Robinson, and others in England, the design principles he evolved for the Winterthur site are unique and have produced a garden that is without equal. Du Pont married his passion for the site with his passion for plants. His focus was on plants that thrived here and were appropriate for the setting. What we have at Winterthur today is the tremendous legacy of plants that survived his aesthetic tests as well as the test of time—plants united in color combinations and seasonal sequences that had never been seen before. This highly successful garden could only have been created by a man thoroughly happy with the process and principles of design he developed. Henry Francis du Pont is an inspiration to all gardenmakers who have come after him.

Postscript

DISCOVERING AMERICA

Letters plied with fair frequency between H. F. du Pont and the leading horticulturists of his day:

> What a perfect way of getting a Ph.D. . . . [This work] will be of the greatest value.
> . . . Wish I could travel around with you.

Du Pont was writing to his friend Henry Skinner, who had decided to search out and catalogue American native azaleas of the eastern and central states as part of his doctoral work for the University of Pennsylvania. During this expedition, Skinner, who later became director of the National Arboretum in Washington, D.C., received an invitation to visit Winterthur upon his return. Du Pont wrote, "I am very keen to hear about all your travels and ask innumerable questions." Skinner's reply provides an engaging sketch of his life as a plant explorer:

> July 8, 1951
>
> Dear Harry:
>
> Many thanks indeed for your kind invitation just found awaiting me at Gatlinburg. . . . [I] will be delighted to accept for lunch, August 21st, until next day. This will be very much looked forward to after such endless tourist courts (good, bad and indifferent) and nights in a sleeping bag!
>
> Collecting has been extremely good, though after 19,000 miles, a little wearing. This happens to be a rare occasion when I am taking a Sunday off to catch up on correspondence, pack plants etc. and rest up a bit after a rather gruelling two nights and days on Gregory Bald in the Smokies Park. Loaded with specimens, plants, blankets, etc. etc. the 4½ mile return hike was pretty strenuous, but the visit was one of the most remarkable I have had. The top of that mountain is a horticulturist's paradise! White arborescens and viscosum have gone wild in interbreeding with a serious red form of calendulaceum resulting in pinks, yellows, golden blotched whites, apricots and reds of all shapes and sizes. . . . [I] have met this sort of situation in a good many places now but the thrill of seeing it for the first time just never wears off.
>
> Am afraid that enough stuff has already gone back to Philadelphia to keep me busy for several years . . . but I believe we will have at the end a quite different picture of what these native azaleas actually are and in what extraordinary ways they are behaving.
>
> My pictures have not yet been developed but if they are any good will bring them along in case you should be interested in a preview.

During June, July, and early August, deciduous native azaleas bloom in luscious colors on Oak Hill. Rhododendron bakeri, the Cumberland azalea, is a favorite luncheon spot for hummingbirds.

NURTURING A FAMILY TRADITION

Jacqueline Hinsley

. . . a family which in at least four generations has made the neighborhood of
Wilmington, Delaware, one of the chief centers of horticulture in the United States.

C. S. SARGENT, *JOURNAL OF THE ARNOLD ARBORETUM* 1924

I have had to cut down large trees to make a place for my garden, but I have not
a fruit tree, and scarcely any seed, to put there. You realize how forlorn
it is to live in the country and to have no garden, no fruit for the children.

E. I. DU PONT TO P. S. DU PONT DE NEMOURS 1803

THE PROMISED LAND

Oh, how happy we would be, my Sophie, away from the volcano on which we live and established in the *promised land*." In the same month, September 1797, that Eleuthère Irénée du Pont (page 40) wrote these words to his wife, his father, Pierre Samuel du Pont de Nemours, had been forced to end his political career in postrevolutionary France. As an editor and publisher, du Pont de Nemours had been an outspoken critic of the Directory's policies. In the chaotic aftermath of a *coup d'état* in Paris on September 4, 1797, du Pont *père* and *fils* were briefly imprisoned, their printing shop ransacked, and the presses wrecked. Convinced that he had no future in his own country, du Pont de Nemours made a decision of far-reaching consequence to his family: he would leave France for America.

He returned to Bois-des-Fossés, the family farm-estate south of Paris, to devote full attention and energy to a prospectus for a rural and commercial enterprise in the United States, "Extrait d'un Plan d'une Opération rurale et commerciale à exécuter dans les Etats-Unis d'Amérique." The commercial part of the scheme, to be directed by his older son, Victor, was essential to its financial success, but the agricultural part, to be managed by the younger son, Irénée, was more in accord with du Pont de Nemours's physiocratic convic-

*E. I. du Pont's garden at
Eleutherian Mills.*

39

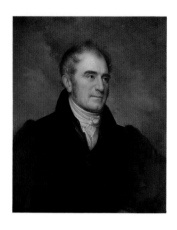

Rembrandt Peale.
Eleuthère Irénée du Pont.
1831. Oil on canvas.

*Rembrandt Peale had been
commissioned by du Pont to
paint his father, Pierre Samuel
du Pont de Nemours, in Paris
in 1808, during the artist's tour
of Europe. In 1813 the two
older du Pont daughters sat for
portraits by Peale in Philadelphia,
and in 1831 their younger
sisters, Eleuthera and Sophie,
journeyed to the city to do the
same "to please Papa." As the
work progressed, du Pont was
persuaded by his daughters to
sit for his portrait also. There
was great excitement when the
paintings arrived. "Our pictures
have all come home. Papa's is
indeed excellent, I never saw a
better one of anyone. Eleu & I
are hung in our parlour, but
Papa has given his to Alfred;
we were sorry that we could not
keep it here. . . . But Papa
wished it, & Alfred of
course has a right to it."*

tion that land is the source of all wealth. The location and geographic advantages of his "rural society" were set down in the prospectus in considerable detail:

> The land will be purchased if possible in upper Virginia and the western counties.
> 1. Because there will be less competition now and more profit in the future than if we settled in Pennsylvania or the state of Newyork.
> 2. Because there is reason to expect more encouragement from the Government.
> 3. Because the mildness of the climate attracts settlers to upper Virginia and the western part of the state.
> 4. Because the navigation of the *Potowmack* and of the *James* river, which is not yet entirely opened and on which work is to be done in 1800 & 1801, will give a prompt and certain increase of value to the land in that neighborhood and will make them the most important of all the beautiful rivers of America.
> 5. Because the central American government will by that time be moved to Wasingthon City, which is being constructed, which will be the most important city in America and which will be ready to receive Congress by 1802 at the latest.
> In upper Virginia the best location is in a beautiful Valley, sixty leagues long by twenty wide, above that of the Shenando situated between the 37th and 39th degrees of latitude sixty leagues from Philadelphia, thirty-five from Baltimore, thirty by the Potowmack from Alexandria and Wasingthon City, forty leagues by the James river from Richmon, the capital of Virginia. More land might be bought beyond the Alleganys, on either bank of the Ohio.
>
> The Valley could support seven hundred thousand inhabitants and does not contain twenty thousand. The soil in this Valley is excellent. It was formerly a lake. It is drained one-third by the James river and two-thirds by the Potowmack of which the south branch is navigable, also by many little streams; there is excellent pasture land. On the border of whatever land is purchased a farm and some cleared land should be set apart. That will be the principal Rural Establishment and the nucleus of later development.

Du Pont de Nemours's plan reflected three decades of personal interest in agrarian reform and in America as a land of social experiment—intellectual orientations widely shared among physiocrats in eighteenth-century France. In his early twenties he had independently formulated the basis of his economic theory. His pamphlets on taxation and free trade in grain brought him to the attention of François Quesnay, *philosophe* and *économiste*. Du Pont de Nemours's publication in 1767 of Quesnay's collected essays, *Physiocratie ou constitution naturelle du gouvernement le plus avantageux au genre humain*, provided the name by which the *économistes* have since been known: physiocrats. The basic tenets of Quesnay and his circle—

that natural law is the governing force of society, that land is the source of wealth, that a single tax should be levied on the net product of the lands, and that agriculture should be free of trade restrictions—coincided entirely with du Pont de Nemours's theories.

Since the purchase in 1774 of Bois-des-Fossés (below), his first landed property, du Pont de Nemours had been putting theory into practice. In less than a decade the small estate was a profitable farm operation. During those years, in which du Pont de Nemours continued to hold government positions in Paris and Versailles, his wife oversaw the seasonal harvests and vintages and managed the sale of hay, wheat and oats, calves, chickens and ducks, and a considerable quantity of wine. Du Pont de Nemours steadily increased the value of his property through improvements and additions.

*Stanley M. Arthurs.
Bois-des-Fossés. 1919.
Oil on canvas.*

This is the artist's conception of the du Pont farm estate near Chevannes, France, as it appeared during the quarter century 1774–99, when it was the family home. The painting was completed from sketches made at Bois-des-Fossés in the summer of 1919, when Arthurs was traveling and painting in Europe.

But how much greater he imagined opportunity to be in the vast virgin lands of America! The proposed location for his enterprise was deeply influenced by Thomas Jefferson's *Notes on the State of Virginia*, first printed privately in a limited English edition in 1785 in Paris and then the next year in a French translation, *Observations sur la Virginie*. Du Pont de Nemours's copy of the French edition was among the books he brought to America. He found a model for his society in a publication in press at his own shop, La Rochefoucauld-Liancourt's *Voyage dans les Etats-Unis d'Amérique fait en 1795, 1796, et 1797*, in which Liancourt detailed such a colony in Genesee, New York, under the direction of a Capt. Charles Williamson.

By 1797, the year of political crisis in du Pont de Nemours's life, there were numerous models available for similar settlements in the United States. Over the next two years father and son continued to gather information and momentum for their transplantation. Publicly du Pont de Nemours, almost sixty years old, worked tirelessly to interest European investors in his Compagnie d'Amérique. Privately he dreamed of the rural society to be established in Virginia.

Irénée took every opportunity to talk with Americans on business in Paris. He learned that land values and the population in Virginia were expected to increase with the anticipated move of the capital to Washington. A discussion with Robert Fulton, American engineer of canals and steamboats, provided him with details about farming, livestock, crops, trade, and transportation in the western lands of Virginia, Kentucky, and Ohio. To Sophie he wrote, "You see, my darling, that with all these details and a thousand others that it would take too long to write, I am as well informed about our future colony as if I had already made the journey."

THE TRANSPLANTATION

In September 1799 the du Ponts were ready to leave Paris: du Pont de Nemours; son Victor with his wife, Josephine, and two children; son Irénée with his wife, Sophie, and three children; stepdaughter Poivre Bureaux de Pusy with her newborn infant; and Sophie's younger brother, Charles Dalmas. (Du Pont de Nemours's second wife, Françoise, and her son-in-law Bureaux de Pusy had sailed for America some months earlier to establish a temporary home.) On October 2 the family left France aboard the *American Eagle*. Overbooked and underprovisioned by a captain whose resources had been exhausted, the unseaworthy vessel did not live up to its name; the voyage took three months. On New Year's Day, 1800, they sighted land; two days later they disembarked at Newport, Rhode Island, to go by packet to

New York, their port of destination, and from there to the country house near Bergen Point, New Jersey, where Mme du Pont and her son-in-law awaited. Josephine described the arrival in an unpublished memoir, "Notre transplantation en Amérique":

> We finished the century at sea, fighting a terrible north-west wind that drove us far from our port. . . . A pleasant home that had been bought by Mr. de Pusy and my mother-in-law received us all. It was beautifully situated, only nine miles from New York on the New Jersey coast, just opposite Staten Island. Papa named the house Good Stay [*Bon Séjour*]. It offered abundant fishing, a superb view, a most healthful climate, as well as the convenience of a neighboring city.

After announcing their arrival to a friend in Charleston, South Carolina, Josephine added, "My father-in-law still counts on a double enterprise, in farming and commerce." While Victor established a commission house in New York, Irénée turned his attention to the gardens and orchards at Good Stay. As their father wrote to Philippe Harmand, a cousin in France, "Victor is excellent for my business, he has a great many ideas and good sense. Irénée is equally good for my gardens. What he has done at Good Stay is astonishing." Pleased with his sons and delighted with the salutary situation of their American home, du Pont de Nemours was optimistic in spite of inflated land prices and dwindling resources. "There is every indication of the complete success of my undertaking," he told Harmand.

Soon after his arrival in America, du Pont de Nemours received an affectionate greeting from his friend Thomas Jefferson:

> I have just heard, my dear friend, of your arrival, and I hasten to welcome you to our shore, where you will at least be free from some of those sources of disquietude which have surrounded you in Europe. . . . The present agonizing state of commerce and the swarms of speculators in money, and in land, would induce me to beseech you to trust nobody, in whatever form they may approach you, till you are fully informed; but your own son [Victor], I am sure, is able to guard you from those who in this, as in every other country, consider the stranger as lawful prey, and watch and surround him on his first arrival.

Jefferson's candid warning was prophetic: there was no cheap land in America for foreign speculators. Land development was out of the question with the limited capital du Pont de Nemours had been able to put together from European investors. Furthermore, the large commission business did not materialize. Faced with the need to generate more

Sophie Madeleine du Pont. "Insect Nests." From Memoir, *vol. 1 [by] Lady Locusta Longhorns, President [Entomological Society]. Watercolor and ink on paper.*

All the du Pont sons and daughters shared an enthusiasm for natural history, the three eldest acting as mentors to their younger siblings. Alfred, a serious student of mineralogy, encouraged "the youngies" to start a "cabinet of curiosities." Victorine and Evelina took them "maying," following French custom, to gather wild-flowers on the first of May in the Brandywine woods—blood-root, anemones, and Virginia bluebells. Henry followed Alfred's example, collecting rocks and minerals; Alexis mounted butterflies. Eleuthera sketched flowers and birds. Sophie was fascinated by the study of insects and their habits; at the age of twelve she organized the Entomological Society, issuing periodic illustrated reports.

Eleuthera du Pont. Magnolia grandiflora. 1821. Watercolor on paper.

capital, du Pont de Nemours outlined several plans for doing business with the governments of France and Spain. Irénée proposed yet another plan: that he be authorized to establish a company for the manufacture of gunpowder, a trade familiar to him. In council at Good Stay, before the end of the first year, the family agreed that Victor and Irénée should return to France to expedite the new projects. On January 5, 1801, they sailed for Europe—Victor to promote the new commercial enterprises and Irénée to obtain machinery and financial support for the powder manufactory.

In Paris Irénée found sufficient support from private investors to proceed with drawing up articles of incorporation for his powder company, E. I. du Pont de Nemours & Co. At the French powder works at Essonnes, where he had studied and worked under Antoine-Laurent Lavoisier, Irénée placed orders for machinery and equipment. Victor met with little success in his talks with high-ranking officials in France and Spain. On his return to the United States he reorganized the commission house in New York under his own name, Victor du Pont de Nemours & Co. The parent company, Du Pont de Nemours, Père et Fils et Cie., to be headquartered in Paris, retained a controlling interest in both Victor's and Irénée's new American companies.

On June 1, 1802, du Pont de Nemours and Françoise returned to France, his dream of a rural society in America unrealized. He carried with him a letter from Irénée to Alexandre Brogniart, director of the Natural History Museum in Paris:

> I received in good time, my dear friend, the letter that you kindly sent me through my brother. . . . I have bought property situated on Brandywine Creek near Wilmington, State of Delaware. The situation is very agreeable and I am busy setting up my gunpowder-mill there. . . . You know, my dear friend, that this was my first profession, and this type of establishment has great advantages here, so that I am feeling very satisfied with my present position. As soon as my business gets established you may rest assured that any leisure I may have will be dedicated to natural history research, which in this country has the double attraction of the variety of the objects as well as their novelty. I am sending you today a small case of [stuffed] birds; I am sorry not to have more for the time being. . . . The State of Delaware where I am going to live, being two degrees of latitude further south, should give us birds and insects of greater variety and more beautiful. . . . Please excuse the haste with which I am writing, but you will readily realize that I am far from being tranquil, when you know that this letter is to be given to you by my father. I do not need to tell you how greatly this separation affects me.

In July 1802 Irénée moved Sophie and their children, Victorine, Evelina, and Alfred, from Good Stay to the site selected for his powder manufactory about four miles north of Wilmington, along Brandywine Creek. Among the household goods shipped on the schooner *Betzy* were "1 cart, 1 plough, 1 harrow, two wheelbarrows, and 1 hand cart." Also on board, du Pont informed a French acquaintance in Wilmington, "are my hunting dogs and some Spanish lambs which I recommend to your care as well as another passenger, Mr. Dalmas, whom I have sent in advance to arrange our lodgings." During their first year in America, Irénée's sister-in-law Josephine had characterized him as a man whose "tastes are simple: botany, hunting, fishing, rural responsibilities. In sum, all the joys one can find in country living and in a happy household are his." It is doubtful that Irénée found time for hunting or fishing during the difficult years of starting a business, but he retained his enthusiasm for botany and natural history and passed it on in full measure to his seven children who, along the rocky banks and wooded hillsides of the Brandywine site, observed, collected, and sketched botanical and entomological specimens (this page).

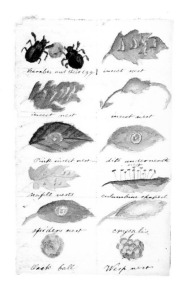

In a printed circular announcing the organization of his company in America, du Pont de Nemours had described his second son, at twenty-nine the youngest of the directors, as a man "who has had much experience of business methods in France in agriculture, manufactures, and the useful arts." At Eleutherian Mills, as Irénée had named his estate on the Brandywine, farming and industry were interdependent and conceptually inseparable. Construction began simultaneously on the mills, house, and barn. In February 1803 the house and barn were completed. The barn was a two-story stone structure with shingle roof, thirty feet wide and forty-five feet long. The first draft animals housed in the barn were the three oxen purchased by du Pont in the fall of 1802 for use during construction and later in the powder yards. Adjacent to the barn stood sheep pens, wagon and carriage sheds, a corncrib, and chicken houses, whose first occupants were one black rooster and three hens of an unusual tufted (topknotted) breed sent to Sophie from Good Stay. Twenty years later the youngest du Pont daughter, Sophie Madeleine, sketched some descendants of "mama's chickens" (page 46).

Magnolia Grandiflora

While the house and barn were under construction, Irénée planted an orchard and cleared more than an acre of land for a garden. Anxious to have fresh fruit and vegetables for his children, he implored his father to obtain from the Jardin des Plantes, where Irénée had studied botany, "some good seeds for the kitchen garden and for the farm, and above all some flower seeds." He also wanted small fruit trees of the best kind: cherries, pears, and

*Sophie Madeleine du Pont.
"Mama's Chickens." 1825.
Pencil on paper.*

*This was sketched in a book of
poetry, literary excerpts, and
drawings belonging to Sophie's
friend "Polly" Simmons.*

*Irénée du Pont. Plan of
orchard and garden. 1804.
Ink on paper.*

*Du Pont's list of pear, apple,
peach, cherry, and plum varieties (in that order) incorporates
Lelieur's list of trees shipped
from France in the spring of
1804 and includes a few
obtained in America. All the
peach trees came from Good
Stay. The orchard plan of the
original drawing is color coded
to the list above. In the garden,
lower right, each parterre shows
a perimeter planting of alternating peach and pear inside the
intersecting paths, the whole
enclosed by similar plantings
outside the paths.*

plums. He enlisted the aid of good friend Louis Lelieur, director of parks and gardens in France, to supply seeds and plants, explaining, "When I began building my establishment here, it was like settling in the back country, no road, no decent house, no garden. You are aware, my friend, that being without a garden was the greatest deprivation; and it is the first thing that occupied my time. I have already planted a hundred excellent peach trees from Good Stay."

Irénée's efforts were rewarded in the spring of 1804. The mills began to manufacture powder, and a huge shipment of seeds and plants, carefully packed by Lelieur, arrived from France in time for spring planting. Three large cases contained grapevines, nut trees, linden and mulberry trees; four varieties of roses; seeds of melons and artichokes; bundles of laven-

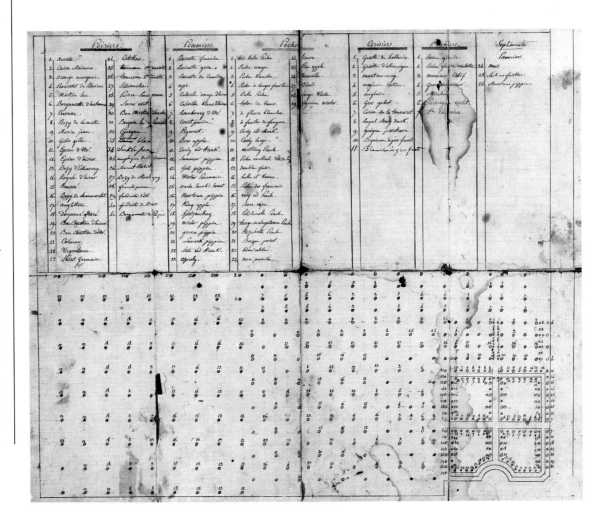

Thomas Mackie Smith.
Bois-des-Fossés. 1846.
Watercolor on paper.

Smith made this painting on a visit to Bois-des-Fossés with his wife, Eleuthera (du Pont) Smith, in August 1846 during a year's tour of Europe. A highlight of the trip was a day spent at Bois-des-Fossés as guests of the Bienaymé family, distant du Pont cousins and owners of the former du Pont estate. While Eleuthera enjoyed her first view of the gardens and grounds of the property so closely associated with her grandfather and her parents, Thomas Mackie sketched the house.

der and tarragon with roots; clumps of violets; raspberries; a collection of seeds for Sophie du Pont's kitchen and flower gardens; and almost two hundred fruit trees, including pear trees grafted on quince that du Pont had requested for training *en quenouille*, a cone-shaped form achieved by staking the branches of young trees to the ground.

Du Pont drew a plan of the orchard and garden incorporating Lelieur's list of trees (opposite). The simple but structured design reflected the influence of French Renaissance garden style: rectilinear beds, or parterres, on either side of a central axis; plants, walls, or fences to form enclosures; and strict control or manipulation of plant material. Irénée took a special interest in grafting and training fruit trees. A significant feature of the garden was a border planting of dwarf fruit trees *en quenouille*.

Du Pont's childhood home may have had more influence than garden theory on the design of the Eleutherian Mills garden. Although topography at the mill site was a determining factor, the completed complex of house, barn, orchard, and garden was remarkably reminiscent of Bois-des-Fossés (above).

Jonas P. Fairlamb. Survey of Eleutherian Mills property. 1812. Ink and watercolor on paper.

The 1812 survey shows a tree-lined entrance road going past the barn and garden to the house, then down a slope by the willow lot bordered by workers' houses to the mills along the creek.

At Eleutherian Mills the machine and the garden coexisted in peaceful harmony. The house stood symbolically between the two—on the one side overlooking the mills and the distant valley, on the other looking out on a more intimate view of the garden and orchard. An 1812 survey (above) shows clearly the configuration of house, barn, and garden, and their proximity to the mills ranged along the creek.

To increase his small flock of sheep Irénée asked his father to send "a couple of Spanish rams and two or three sheep . . . for my little farm." In 1805 he had the unexpected good fortune of acquiring Don Pedro (opposite), believed to be the first full-blooded merino ram introduced into North America and brought from France under Irénée's care in 1801 for Alexandre Delessert, a French banker with a farm on the Hudson near Kingston, New York. Don Pedro was pastured at Good Stay with the du Ponts' small flock of ewes before being sent on to Delessert's farm. When Delessert leased his farm and sold off his stock in 1805, Irénée's agent bought the ram at auction for $60.

To encourage sheepraising in the Wilmington area and to improve the quality of local flocks, du Pont offered Don Pedro's services to neighboring farmers without fee. He also offered to buy all the half and three-quarter merinos they might wish to sell. At the same time he engaged in buying, selling, and trading with other prominent sheep breeders, including Chancellor Robert Livingston, former American minister to France; William Thornton, architect of the Capitol and superintendent of the Patent Office; and Philadelphians Callender Irvine and James Mease. He continued urgent and frequent appeals to his father to send merino sheep from France, assuring him that a merino was "one of the best speculations that could be made in this country." In April 1808 one of Don Pedro's offspring sold for $40. Six months later Irénée wrote his father that he could get $400 to $500 for his first- and second-generation merino lambs. By this time he was planning to build a woolen factory across the creek from his mills and to persuade his brother Victor to engage in the woolen industry as manager of the factory. He urged his father, as he had done many times before, to come back to America and join them: "Imagine on the opposite banks our two factories, our two houses, our two families—and you with us."

Engrav'd for the Archives of Useful Knowledge.

G. Murray sc.

DON PEDRO

The Property of E. I. Dupont Esq.

G. Murray. Don Pedro. Copperplate engraving. From James Mease, ed., Archives of Useful Knowledge (Philadelphia: David Hogan, 1811), frontispiece.

This engraving of Don Pedro accompanies the discourse "Observations on Sheep," which appeared in Archives. Ostensibly written by the editor, the piece was in fact authored by Irénée du Pont, who chose to be anonymous. "I beg and trust," he wrote to Mease, "that if you Publish you will be so good as to take the trouble to put it in better english and be careful not to let any gallicism remain. . . . The compliments paid to Pedro will have better effect and do him more honor coming from you than from me."

Inflated prices and speculative trading in merinos continued through 1809, when merino mania, triggered by the patriotic effort to end the British monopoly on textiles, had run its course. Future profits in sheep would come from woolgrowing for manufacture, not for speculation. Du Pont was in the vanguard, with a woolen mill already under construction in the winter of 1810. Anticipating flocks of several hundred sheep to supply the new factory, he looked around for additional grazing lands. The 65 acres at Eleutherian Mills, purchased from Jacob Broom in 1802, were adequate for Irénée's "little farm," but most of the site was in use for mills, millraces, roads, and willow lots (for charcoal used in making powder). The addition of a contiguous 29-acre tract, for which du Pont made an option agreement with Broom's son in 1810, would not make a significant difference in available pasture- and farmland. In January 1810 du Pont bought a farm of 180 acres from the estate of Nathan Simmons. In a letter to his father some months later, he wrote:

> I bought last spring a fertile farm of 180 acres with enough good land to put an improved flock there under the direction of an excellent man who was one of my workers for eight years and who would like to retire to farm; in giving him a little interest in the flock I have attached him to the project; this farm can maintain at present 500 sheep. . . . my calculation is that the production of lambs pays for the food and the expenses of the shepherd. . . . I was looking for a farm to rent last spring when I found for sale this one that I have named *Merino farm*, which is only a mile from our home in a very pretty location and which cost me $23 per acre, or to be more accurate, will cost me since I gave only a quarter in cash and will pay the remainder when the children, now eight years old will be over twenty-one. This sale although made by minors and their guardian is legal, having been approved by the court of justice.

On April 6, 1811, du Pont and John Hirons signed articles of agreement for the sale of a farm containing 169 acres; this was the area known as Clenny. The sale was completed on October 7, 1812. That same year Irénée purchased from James Russell a small tract of land, 11 acres, bordering the Simmons farm and Kennett Turnpike. In 1818 he bought from Margaret Campbell 84 acres adjoining and connecting the other three tracts. These four properties, acquired between 1810 and 1818, constituted the farm that became Winterthur.

By the terms of the purchase of Nathan Simmons's farm, his widow and two children received a house on the property and a

Sophie Madeleine du Pont. "Going to Pol's." 1827. Ink on paper.

"On Thursday Tat [Eleuthera] Lil [Alexis] and I determined to go and spend the day at Pol's. . . . Papa insisted on our all three going in his gig, Riley leading the horse—we presented a truly comic appearance, Tat and I on the seat; I, loaded with portfolios, crayon cases etc. for drawing; Tat, with a bundle of stockings to darn and a story she took for us to read— Between us, aloft in awful state on a barrel of pears and melons, sat Alexis, armed with the net to catch insects, which floated like a green pennen in triumph over the horse's head." From Sophie's diary, August 30, 1827.

lot for a cow. The younger child, a daughter named Mary Elizabeth (called Polly), and Irénée's daughter Sophie were childhood friends, sending notes back and forth by the farm wagon. A visit to the merino farm ("going to Pol's") was a favorite day's outing for the four youngest du Pont children born at Eleutherian Mills between 1806 and 1816: Eleuthera, Sophie, Henry, and Alexis.

The "excellent man" who managed the Simmons farm was Billy Martin. He, with his wife, Fanny, had kept a boarding house for the powdermen at Eleutherian Mills. Irénée had a house built for the Martins at the Simmons farm, which in time came to be known as the Martin farm.

On his newly acquired farmlands, Irénée planted large quantities of clover, orchard grass, rye, oats, wheat, and barley and experimented with growing millet, a cereal grain from Europe used in America for fodder. He submitted his findings, "On the Culture of Millet," to James Mease, a Philadelphia physician, agriculturalist, and editor of *Archives of Useful Knowledge*. Du Pont's essay did not appear in print, but a manuscript copy survives, in his hand, signed "A Delaware farmer."

Agricultural and horticultural interests brought Irénée du Pont into an informal circle of prominent Delawareans—doctors, lawyers, printers, publishers, gentlemen farmers, and entrepreneurs—who in the early years of the Republic were drawn into the cultural, social, and economic sphere of Philadelphia. They came together through mutual interests in land and agriculture, plant experimentation, animal husbandry, botany, and horticulture. They exchanged ideas in the journals and proceedings of scientific and agricultural societies. Du Pont became a member of the American Philosophical Society in 1807, the Philadelphia Society for Promoting Agriculture in 1808, and the Pennsylvania Horticultural Society in 1830.

A strong Anglo-American horticultural tradition prevailed in Philadelphia, reflecting eighteenth-century Quaker roots and producing outstanding gardens and arboreta. European botanists and naturalists observing and collecting American flora had long gravitated to Philadelphia. Many of them—French botanists François André Michaux, Constantine Rafinesque, and Auguste Plée; French naturalists Charles Alexandre Lesueur and Jean Baptiste Leschenault; and Portuguese naturalist José Francisco Corréa da Serra—visited Eleutherian Mills to botanize in the Brandywine woods and to enjoy the cosmopolitan ambience of the du Pont home. Through these various connections, Irénée became acquainted with Philadelphia nurserymen who were an integral part of the horticultural network. Even before 1810 he was buying regularly from Bartram's Gardens, David Landreth, and

Overleaf: A view of Eleutherian Mills house and barn with the restored garden in the right foreground.

Invoice from McMahon & Co.
to E. I. du Pont, Esq. 1834.

Bernard McMahon. Although his garden remained essentially French in character through-out the nineteenth century, it underwent a gradual Americanization as native plants sup-planted or supplemented the original varieties shipped from France. The quarter century from 1810 to 1834 marked the beginning of the uniquely Franco-American nature of the du Pont gardens in the Brandywine Valley.

Throughout the three decades of his lifetime on the Brandywine, Irénée du Pont consistently demonstrated a passionate belief in man's connection with the land. He also saw clearly the interdependence of manufactures and agriculture, sharing with other Brandywine millowners the belief that the establishment of manufactures in rural areas "accomplishes magic effects . . . enrich[ing] the country and the farmers." Irénée du Pont thus left a dual legacy: an industrial company that bears his name and a family tradition of agriculture and horticulture.

THE SECOND GENERATION

Of du Pont's three sons, it was Henry, the first son born in America, who was destined to continue the agricultural and horticultural tradition on the Brandywine. Soon after his son's birth on August 8, 1812, Irénée predicted in a letter to his father in France: "This little one may live to be head of our American family; I want him to have a good name and so I beg you to choose it for him." But for the war with England, the future head of the du Pont family might have been called Aristides, the name that arrived too late. After three months with no response, his parents called him Henry, "a good French name."

Like his father, Henry combined an inherent love of the land with an innate ability for managing a business. As senior partner of E. I. du Pont de Nemours & Co. for four decades, 1850 to 1889, and lifelong occupant of the house at Eleutherian Mills, he was ideally positioned to maintain a farm and garden way of life at the original mill site and to continue the acquisition of additional farmlands.

Henry's passionate love of the land had also been shaped by an idyllic childhood in the natural environs of his home, which, at ten years of age, he reluctantly left for military schooling. After ten years at Mount Airy Military College in Germantown, Pennsylvania, and the United States Military Academy at West Point, followed by a brief tour of duty, Henry resigned his commission as second lieutenant and returned to the Brandywine, at his father's request, to take his place in the family business. Although he is recalled as "the General"—with all that the title connotes of unbending authority and stern austerity—Henry du Pont had never been drawn to a military career. (The title derives from his reactivated service during the Civil War as major general in command of Delaware's Home Guards.)

Only four months after Henry left the army Irénée died suddenly, on October 31, 1834, while on a business trip to Philadelphia. Three years later, in the final settling of the estate, the 450-acre farm property on Kennett Turnpike, which had been inherited jointly by his seven children, was offered for sale. In April 1837, Henry's sister Evelina and her husband, Jacques Antoine Bidermann, a partner in the du Pont company, purchased the property from the other heirs for $16,000. After deciding to make it their home, they named the farm Winterthur, for the Swiss town that was Bidermann's ancestral home. While a new farmhouse was being built, to be occupied by the Bidermanns until the main house could be designed and completed, they took an extended trip to France. During the next two years, Henry and his older brother Alfred oversaw the Winterthur construction and carried on extensive correspondence with their brother-in-law to answer his many questions about soil, crops, and livestock. In a letter to Alfred dated April 6, 1839, Antoine thanked Henry "for the details . . . on *Durham cattle and other livestock*. From what he says I think that if I want full bred cows, it will be better to import them myself than to buy them in America."

Wheat cultivation and cattle breeding were Henry's consuming agricultural interests. He gained national as well as local recognition for his scientific experimentation with all varieties of wheat suitable to Delaware's latitude: the Wilmington *Daily Republican* noted that "his hundreds of acres of wheat yielded thirty to sixty bushels per acre." The development of outstanding du Pont cattle herds, for which Winterthur later became famous, began with Henry du Pont at Eleutherian Mills. The inventory of Irénée's estate had listed seven cows and four calves, all Holsteins crossed with Durham bulls. From this small herd Henry steadily increased the number and quality. By the 1840s the "du Pont herd of Durhams" was a prominent feature at the fairs of the Agricultural Society of New Castle County.

Irénée also left ten carriage and riding horses, with fourteen draft horses for hauling powder. That number had doubled in less than ten years. To accommodate the increasing number of livestock, in the 1840s Henry enlarged the barn built by his father to twice its original size (this page). In 1844, a year after expanding the old barn, he built a much larger new one, located near the home of his sister Eleuthera and her husband, Dr. Thomas Mackie Smith.

Theophilus P. Chandler. Eleutherian Mills barn. 1873. Ink wash on paper.

The barn sketched by Henry du Pont's son-in-law Theophilus Chandler in 1873, essentially unchanged since Henry enlarged it in the 1840s, appears the same today.

The new barn housed cattle and provided storage space for hay and grain, leaving the old barn for horses and vehicles. Twice the new barn was badly damaged by fire: in 1851, when it was rebuilt, and again in 1889, during an outbreak of incendiary barn burnings in the Brandywine area. Describing the 1851 fire to her husband, Samuel Francis, Henry's sister Sophie noted that "besides the loss and inconvenience which are great, this was his hobby, his recreation from business, to attend to his farm and cattle."

Henry's horticultural interests ran more to landscaping than gardening, with a particular fondness for evergreens. "We are in the midst of improvements," his wife, Louisa (née Gerhard), reported in 1857 to their nineteen-year-old son, Henry Algernon, a student at West Point, who shared Henry's love of trees.

> Your father has levelled the ground below the office and thrown the cowpen into one enclosure. . . . He has sent for a good many evergreens—cedars, silver pines, Norway spruce, a few rapidly growing maples, etc. These will be sufficient to fill the vacancies on the hill and to plant the new enclosure. I wish you could be here this spring and I am always thinking how much interest and pleasure it would give you to superintend our improvements.

Louisa du Pont was an enthusiastic and knowledgeable gardener. She supervised the gardeners at Eleutherian Mills, exchanged plants with her sisters-in-law at their Brandywine estates, Nemours, Hagley, Louviers, and Winterthur, and excused her husband's seeming lack of interest in ornamental horticulture. "Henry . . . is really very fond of flowers but has not the time to think of them. The family love of flowers will be, I hope, continued in my children." That hope was fulfilled. The second generation of children growing up at Eleutherian Mills was as devoted to gardening as the first. Daughter Victorine, recalling the garden of her childhood, felt that "the great charm of this garden, like all those that the hand of time has touched, was its luxuriance, and the reminder everywhere that age alone could produce its wonderful effect." The hand of time was not solely reponsible for the changed appearance of Irénée's garden during the half century it was tended by Henry and Louisa and their sons and daughters: a rose garden, vine-covered trellises, grape arbors, and boxwood borders clearly reflected the Victorian garden aesthetic of the years 1840 to 1890 (this page).

In 1867 Henry purchased the Winterthur farm. Four years earlier Evelina had died and Antoine Bidermann had returned to France, appointing Henry and cousin Charles I. du Pont coadministrators of the farm that his meticulous management had turned into "one of the most productive . . . in the State." Bidermann died in 1865, leaving the estate to his

Theophilus P. Chandler. Eleutherian Mills garden. 1873. Ink wash on paper.

View of the mature garden, looking southeast toward Brandywine Creek. The cold frame and toolshed are in the left foreground; the summerhouse is beyond the pump. The woman in the foreground is probably the artist's wife, Sophie (du Pont) Chandler, daughter of Henry and Louisa du Pont.

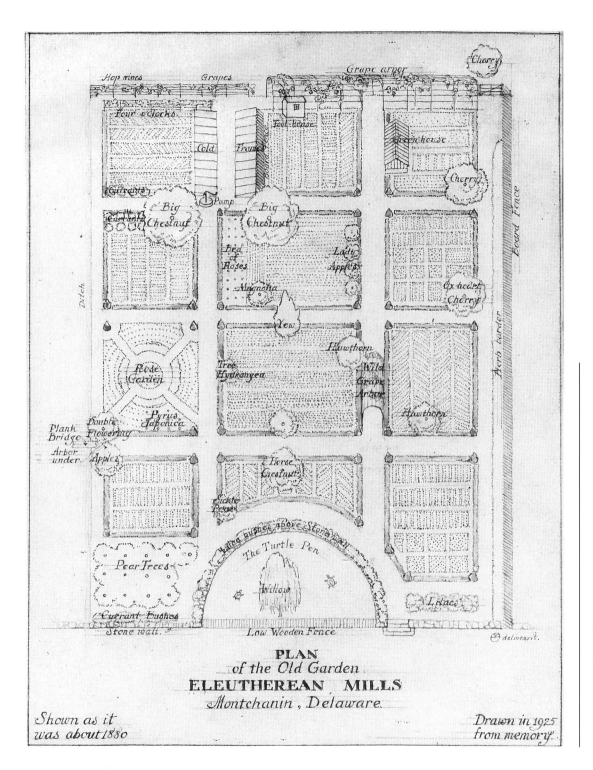

Hop vines · Grapes · Grape arbor · Cherry

Four o'clocks

Cold · Frames · Tool house · Greenhouse

Currants

Currants · Big Chestnut · Pump · Big Chestnut · Cherry

Bed of Roses · Lady Apples

Magnolia · Ox-heart Cherry

Yew

Rose Garden · Tree Hydrangea · Hawthorn · Wild Grape Arbor · Hawthorn

Plank Bridge · Double Flowering · Pyrus Japonica

Arbor under · Apple

Horse Chestnut

Sickle Pears

Laltas bushes above Stone wall

Pear Trees · The Turtle Pen · Willow

Currant Bushes · Lilacs

Stone wall · Low Wooden Fence

Ditch · Board Fence · Herb border

delineavit

PLAN
of the Old Garden
ELEUTHEREAN MILLS
Montchanin, Delaware.

Shown as it was about 1880

Drawn in 1925 from memory

*Victorine (du Pont) Foster.
Plan of the old garden. 1925.
Ink on paper.*

This plan shows the garden
at Eleutherian Mills in the
1880s as recalled by Victorine
(du Pont) Foster. Excavations
in the 1970s revealed a discrep-
ancy between the drawing and
the actual garden. The path to
the right should be centered over
the half circle identified as the
turtle pen. The four parterres in
the lower right are the original
garden shown in du Pont's
1804 plan. Over the years the
garden expanded south and
west, gradually taking over part
of the orchard. The plan for the
restored garden, now open to
the public, was drawn in 1972
by William H. Frederick, Jr.,
landscape architect.

*Col. Henry Algernon du Pont
in dress uniform.*

*Henry Algernon du Pont had a
distinguished military career.
Possessed of an orderly and inci-
sive mind, he enjoyed taking
command and assuming responsibility. After graduating first in
his class at West Point in 1861
with a commission as second
lieutenant in the Corps of
Engineers, he saw active service
throughout the Civil War. In
March 1898 he was awarded the
Congressional Medal of Honor
and was made lieutenant colonel
"for distinguished gallantry and
voluntary exposure to the enemy's
fire at a critical moment" in the
Battle of Cedar Creek. He
received his commission in March
1865. After the war, although
his father and uncle Lammot
du Pont urged him to leave the
army and join the company, he
continued a military career
until his marriage.*

only son and heir, James Irénée Bidermann, who since 1837 had made his home in France. When word came that James planned to sell Winterthur, Henry made an offer to buy the farm. He had always felt a strong attachment for the property; it had belonged to his father, then to his sister and brother-in-law. He had no intention of making Winterthur his own residence, nor did he have any assurance in 1867 that either of his two sons would ever live there. But as Henry explained to his nephew in France, "In regard to your landed property, the Winterthur Estate . . . I have decided to make you an offer for it, not for myself . . . but to keep the property in the family, and with the possibility, that hereafter, it might be available to one of my two sons."

In March 1867 Henry received the deed of sale for which he paid $44,500. Throughout the spring and summer, when the Italian stonemasons employed at the mills had "no large jobs on hand," Henry put them to work building walls and fences at Winterthur, a practice he continued for many years. In October of that year, following one of his frequent morning visits to the farm, Henry reported to Henry Algernon that "everything looked well and the house is in wonderful good repair considering the long time it has been untenanted." A year later Louisa told their son, "Your father . . . seems to be able to take the charge of that large place as easily & naturally as he does everything else. We often go there & love the place very much. It is neglected & overgrown with weeds but the shrubbery is not destroyed & one recognizes everywhere the plants your Aunt Lina loved so much."

In the autumn of 1873 Henry Algernon asked Mary Pauline Foster of New York to marry him and soon afterward accepted his father's offer to make Winterthur his home because, he said, "it would be hard on Pauline not to have a settled home." They were married in New York on July 15, 1874, and sailed for England in September. In December, while in France, Henry Algernon submitted his resignation from the army, effective March 1, 1875.

While the young couple toured Europe for a year, Henry once again found himself making Winterthur ready for new occupants and overseeing the necessary renovations. One of the first improvements was the installation of stone gateposts on Kennett Turnpike, "which," as he wrote to his son, "will last forever." In early spring Henry's gardener began "ridding out the tangle" of the overgrown garden, repairing potting beds and cisterns, and putting the old greenhouse in order. Asparagus and strawberry beds were planted, grapevines started, and dwarf fruit trees put in. In October 1875 Henry Algernon and Pauline returned to Wilmington in time to see "the woods [at Winterthur] still full of flowers—fringed gentians, asters & golden rods—and bright with their gold & crimson dyes." They moved into their home on April 26, 1876.

Henry retained ownership of Winterthur until his death on August 8, 1889, at which time he was said to be the largest landholder in New Castle County. During his twenty-two years as owner of the Winterthur property, he had increased its acreage from the original 445 to 1,135. His many improvements in the last decades of his life were critical to its future development as a farm estate. By the terms of his will, Winterthur became the property of his son Henry Algernon.

CONTINUING A TRADITION

When Henry Algernon du Pont inherited Winterthur in 1889, it had been his home since 1876, the year after he returned to civilian life to join the powder company. After becoming a member of the firm, he had taken his place beside his father in the company office located between the house and the barn, overlooking the Brandywine river. The small stone building, overrun by his father's pet greyhounds, was closely associated with Henry Algernon's recollections of growing up at Eleutherian Mills.

Henry Algernon du Pont. Sketch. 1852. Pencil on paper.

Henry Algernon's lively little sketch of a heifer and two grey-hounds, drawn when he was fourteen years old, was presented to his aunt Sophie on her birthday, September 18, 1852.

For the first twelve years of his life, before going away to school, Henry Algernon had enjoyed a carefree childhood reminiscent of the early years of his father's generation in the same surroundings. At Eleutherian Mills, at the center of an enclave of aunts, uncles, and cousins, he had developed a strong sense of family. In later years, encouraged by his aunt Sophie du Pont, he became the du Pont family genealogist and biographer.

As a boy, Henry Algernon had shown considerable talent for sketching familiar scenes and objects: landscapes, horses, cattle, and, scattered throughout, the ubiquitous greyhounds (page 59 and below). The subject matter of these early sketches suggests the more serious pursuits of his later years at Winterthur, where greyhounds continued to be a part of the landscape.

Between 1876 and 1889 Henry Algernon concentrated his efforts at Winterthur on horticultural improvements to the gardens, greenhouses, and lawns; tree plantings; and architectural changes to the house. After his father's death in 1889, Henry Algernon became more involved in the management and development of the farm operation. Like his father and uncle, Antoine Bidermann, he took a serious interest in breeding dairy cattle and, like so many members of his family, also became a knowledgeable and enthusiastic gardener. His respect for the land and appreciation for its natural beauty had begun at Eleutherian Mills, but it was at Winterthur that Henry Algernon continued a farm and garden tradition rooted in eighteenth-century France, transplanted to America, and nurtured by four generations of du Ponts.

Henry Algernon du Pont. Sketch. 1850. Pencil and watercolor on paper.

Inscribed to Aunt Sophie from her nephew Henry, January 1, 1850. The du Ponts followed the French custom of visiting friends and exchanging gifts on New Year's Day.

Postscript

NATURE AND NURTURE

Henry Algernon du Pont, perhaps emulating his father, met the world with a demeanor rather formal and reserved. The following letter, written to his son, Henry Francis, when young Harry first found himself at boarding school, reveals less-obvious aspects of Henry Algernon's temperament as well as a glimpse of family life at their home and the continuity of family traditions.

19 October 1893

Mon cher, cher Enfant,

Your letter of last Saturday was received . . . and I could not help thinking a great deal about you all day long.

You must know how thoroughly I appreciate your feelings and how much I wish that it were in my power to make you feel immediately happy and comfortable at school!

Remember that I have been also in a position like yours and your grandfather, too, before me. He went to the military school at Mount Airy in 1822 he was only ten years old!

I want to tell you how much pleasure it has given me to find you have been so brave and manly in all your letters to Louise, Aunt Victorine and others.

Keep up your courage, my dear Harry, and try absolutely to interest yourself in your surroundings—in your lessons and in the companionship of the other boys—and this will make your new life easier for you.

You say nothing about having played ball or tennis and I trust that you are taking part in the games with the others. When you write tell me something in regard to this as well as about your studies. I am very anxious to know how you are getting on in your classes.

[Your sister] Louise began her lessons this morning with the new governess. She sends her best love as well as Uncles William and Augustus who leave us tomorrow morning.

Mama sends a thousand affectionate messages and bids me tell you that she despatched a basket of fruit to you by express this morning.

This is the anniversary of the Battle of Cedar Creek, one of the most important episodes of my life, and it pleases me to think that my first letter to you should date from today.

Goodbye, dearest Harry. Think often of all the advice I have given you. Write *fully* and *freely* and believe me always

Your loving father,
H. A. du Pont

ON BECOMING A GARDENER

Denise Magnani

Train up a child in the way he should go:
and when he is old he will not depart from it.

PROVERBS 22:6

I have always loved flowers and had a garden as a child, . . .
and if you have grown up with flowers and really seen them you can't help
to have unconsciously absorbed an appreciation of proportion,
color, detail, and material.

H. F. DU PONT 1962

Winterthur in the late nineteenth century was, in the Jamesian phrase, "a great good place." The du Ponts were diligent stewards of their land. To create Winterthur, three generations had stitched together a vast patchwork of meadows, forests, farms, and houses with a coherent system of country roads. The tenant farmers tended their crops according to the latest principles of scientific agriculture. The bustling interactions of their growing families imparted to the estate the feeling of a small village.

Winterthur was the "settled home" that Henry Algernon du Pont had promised to provide for Mary Pauline Foster when she accepted his offer of marriage in 1873. She had been raised in New York State in a family whose values included the close connection with the land that the du Ponts embraced. She wanted to work beside her husband and raise their children in a country place.

On the last day of June 1876 she wrote to one of her cousins in New York: "We have been in our house for two months and of course we have been very busy, I, inside the house, and my husband out-of-doors. There are so many trees around the house that we had a great many cut which is a great improvement. The woods are beautiful and filled with berries, and several springs."

*Path and narcissus grove.
c. 1908.*

Daffodils along the path (later known as the March Walk) are lined up in rigid clumps, in contrast to the more naturalistic drifts higher up on the bank that are part of the narcissus grove inspired by William Robinson's writings. This photograph captures a time of transition in the Winterthur landscape when conventional plantings such as the "old-fashioned daffodils in little groups here and there" coexisted with the beginnings of a coherent, expressive use of materials.

Like the other du Pont Brandywine estates, Winterthur provided Henry Algernon ample opportunities to explore his interests in agriculture, horticulture, and the natural sciences. Although he felled some trees to open views around the house, he spent far more time preserving notable specimens. He surveyed the second-growth woods on the property, searching for any survivors of the primeval forest that had escaped the woodsman's ax.

For the young couple, "putting down roots" included actual planting. Within a few years of arriving with Pauline, Henry Algernon sited a grove of saucer magnolias (*M.* x *soulangiana*) and further enlarged the Bidermann garden plots. Eventually he added 900 acres to the estate, 430 of them woodland.

The couple soon established a balanced routine. Each morning Henry Algernon went to Eleutherian Mills to work in the company office overlooking the Brandywine river. In 1879, after becoming president of the Wilmington and Northern Railroad, he usually attended to railroad matters in the afternoon while Pauline managed the household. They often socialized with their many du Pont relatives; Winterthur became a favorite spot for family gatherings.

Pauline's fondest wish was to have a family of her own. Her greatest sorrow was that only two of her seven children survived infancy. Her daughter, Louise Evelina, born August 3, 1877, was an affectionate and joyful baby. Her son was born on May 27, 1880. Henry Algernon's mother, whom they called Bonne Maman, wrote to a friend, "You will be very glad to hear we have a beautiful boy at Winterthur. He was born, as all the other children were—prematurely . . . before the doctor could reach Winterthur. . . . The baby has been gaining one pound a week. . . . It only weighed 4½ lbs. or less when it was born." The infant was named Henry Francis du Pont and was called Harry (page 66).

An acquaintance of Pauline's described her as "the kindest person I ever met." She lavished her children with love and attention and included them in the daily activities of the estate. Louise and Harry came to see Winterthur through her eyes. Harry recalled that his mother thought of Winterthur not "as a show place" but rather as "a place where people live who love the country." It was a six-mile trek to Wilmington; they tried to be as self-sufficient as possible. Louise and Harry were educated at home during their early years.

Pauline loved flowers and taught her children to garden in the enlarged Bidermann plot. To reach the garden, the three would-be horticulturists had to follow a narrow path from the house down a steep, wooded slope (page 66). Coming upon the neat rows of flowers and vegetables ripening in the sun, admiring mother's roses, Harry's peas, or Louise's beans must have seemed more like fun than a lesson, but it was one learned by heart.

The pilgrims who founded Plymouth Colony saw the North American forest as a "waste and howling wilderness." By the mid nineteenth century, Henry David Thoreau was living at Walden Pond; his mentor, Ralph Waldo Emerson, counseled, "In the woods, we return to reason and faith." There are twenty-six miles of roads and woodland paths at Winterthur, most of them laid out by Henry Algernon du Pont before 1900.

Left: Henry Francis du Pont. c. 1887.

Harry loved the freedom of the outdoors. As a child, he had "the run of the place . . . the farm too" and learned the lessons that only repeated, intimate contact with nature can teach. For this studio portrait, however, he had to be content with the photographer's painted backdrop.

Right: Pauline du Pont with her children, Louise and Harry. c. 1890.

Of his mother's influence on his interest in horticulture, Harry said, "She loved flowers . . . that's the reason I got so interested in them too."

Winterthur house from the southeast. c. 1885.

It all started here. This photograph shows the path winding down a wooded slope to the garden plots, cold frames, and small greenhouse. Harry was able to protect his "mother's crabapple," in the center of the picture, through several renovations to the site. In the 1960s the tree finally succumbed to old age.

Gardening was a passion the siblings shared throughout their long lives and one they always associated with their mother.

The du Ponts both strove to instill an appreciation of nature in their children. Pauline praised their children's gardening efforts and made a game of gathering wildflowers to decorate the house. Henry Algernon's educational attentions bore a slightly different stamp. Louise recalled years later: "Father would take Harry and me by the hand and walk through the gardens with us, and if we couldn't identify the flowers and plants by their botanical names, we were sent to bed without our suppers." After all, being conversant with the natural world was required of all educated persons—certainly all du Ponts!

The lives of several generations of the family were closely intertwined; the children had almost a second home with their grandparents. The most vivid descriptions of the daily rhythms at Eleutherian Mills were written in 1955 by Louise:

> As soon as I was old enough I used to go over every afternoon on my pony to see Grandmama, accompanied by our faithful William. When I grew older I used to drive myself in a pony cart, but I never missed going every afternoon.
>
> From 1880 to 1889 when my father and mother went away from Winterthur for any reason, Harry and I were always sent down to Grandmama's to stay, and that is how I came to know my grandfather so well. Otherwise I only saw him at Sunday dinner when there were so many people at the table that my only contact was a peck on each cheek. But when I lived there in the house it was quite different. I always breakfasted with him and his cat Minette at seven o'clock. We all three had the same breakfast—pieces of bread broken in a bowl of milk and big glasses of milk to drink. Minette, I imagine, skipped the latter. . . .
>
> My grandfather and grandmother were married in Chester in 1837. I always felt and still do that she was one of the most marvelous people that the world has ever known. Fifty years after the date of their marriage they celebrated their golden wedding, which was a great event in my childhood. . . . Harry and I and my French nurse picked an enormous number of yellow daisies which my mother had planted the spring before in preparation for this date. We made them into a huge wreath. . . .
>
> I shall never forget the music, the crowds, the unlimited ice cream, all very different from my usual life. I sat near Grandmama all the time. Having been named for her and being the oldest girl in the family, I always considered myself "Pet 1," which I really think I was.

"Pet 1" grew up to be very much like her grandmother—generous, self-confident, quick-witted, and sociable. Her brother was more shy and reserved, traits his father

Henry Algernon saw in "my father, Henry du Pont, . . . a man of even temperament and not given to enthusiastic personal comment (in disposition Harry resembles him very strongly)."

LESSONS

Henry Algernon was a natural teacher who could turn almost anything that happened at Winterthur into a lesson in aesthetics, science, or practical farm management. There was always a need to design, or redesign, bridges, culverts, dams, steps, walkways, retaining walls, and small buildings. After inheriting Winterthur in 1889, he laid out miles of gently curving roads designed for those on horseback or in a carriage. He maintained a stable and carriage long after automobiles had become popular and emulated his father's practice of visiting the different farms each day in his gig. Harry often accompanied him, and as they glided through the landscape, one beautiful scene after another appeared before their eyes, providing the perfect backdrop for impromptu lectures on natural history.

Harry had a model for a humanistic management style when he watched his father direct the varied activities of the workmen and farmers. As the du Pont family genealogist, Henry Algernon was aware of his family's accomplishments and had strong feelings about its responsibility to society. From his earliest days, Harry was imbued with a sense of his obligation to continue the du Pont family's values and traditions.

Harry and Louise had the run of the estate. Their mother told them, "Play anywhere. Play in the meadow." In the 1880s, fields, old fields, pioneer hardwoods, and second-growth forests—the stages of forest succession—were the playgrounds for all the children who lived at Winterthur. (Between 100 and 200 workers and their families lived there at any one time.) Harry and Louise had little need to romanticize their childhood or the beauty of the landscape. The reality that surrounded them as they grew up had enough lyricism and mystery to last a lifetime. And they never forgot it.

When Harry du Pont was eighty-two years old, an interviewer asked him about the source of his love for Winterthur. His answer was an evocative image called up from a childhood idyll: "We had a big oak tree in front of the house. It's not there any longer and I remember the time I found a hummingbird's nest on a branch. It was quite near the ground, of course—a big branch and a little bit of a thing."

A VERY YOUNG COLLECTOR

The tiny nest and its fragile contents are long gone, but a few shards of 100-year-old speckled, sky blue eggshells are among Winterthur's most precious, if not most valuable, holdings.

Harry made a collection of birds' eggs as a boy and came upon the forgotten cache in one of the barns about seventy-five years later. The interviewer who had questioned du Pont at age eighty-two was Harlan Phillips, on a mission from the Smithsonian Institution's Archives of American Art to discover something of the "aesthetic and collecting impulses" of one of the great collectors and gardeners of his generation.

To hear Harry tell it, growing up with flowers made him a gardener. As for the collecting, he said he "must have been born with it," as he "always collected minerals, bird's eggs, stamps, etc." Phillips doggedly probed and gently prodded and gradually extracted a few revealing details. As du Pont reported, "Everyone collected in those days." (He was undoubtedly also "born with" his laconicism, courtesy of grandfather du Pont.) Harry enlisted his family's help in completing his early accumulations. Before Christmas 1895 he wrote to his parents, "If anyone does not know what to give me, they can give me some money and I will get some stamps as there are a good many that I want."

From C. J. Maynard, Eggs of North American Birds *(Boston, 1890), frontispiece.*

Museums as we know them were an invention of the late eighteenth and early nineteenth centuries. Many visitors to these institutions were inspired to amass their own collections of curiosities or mount private natural history displays. Charles Darwin published *Origin of Species* in 1859. Throughout the century, data concerning the relationships among species were figuratively and literally being unearthed as expeditions of scientists discovered fossil remains of previous inhabitants of the Far West. Painters, poets, and the authors of a spate of travel and guide books declared the American landscape to be beautiful, picturesque, romantic, magnificent, and sublime. Tourists flocked to the new national parks.

Against this backdrop Harry approached his hobbies with an almost scientific methodology. He adopted his father's habit of careful observation and precise notation, keeping a diary about his dog Shec and recording the number of eggs laid by his Brahma hens. Early on he showed the determination and perseverance necessary in any successful collector. He raised terriers and wrote to his parents, "This is no passing fancy. I do not mean to quit until I have raised a prize winner." For his thirteenth birthday Bonne Maman gave Harry a beautifully illustrated book, *Eggs of North American Birds*. She wanted to encourage his interest in the world around him, a world which, that same year, became much larger.

At age thirteen Harry was enrolled in Groton School, a boys' preparatory academy forty miles northwest of Boston. His father's idea was reasonable—that Harry become "a good, useful, honorable man appreciating the duty he owes to the community in which he lives and to his fellow men." Eventually Henry Algernon's hopes were fulfilled, and, after forty years or so, even Harry admitted that the experience had probably done him some good. At the time the separation provoked an intense reaction. His parents might just as well have tossed a fledgling from the nest, tearing him from everything that gave meaning and comfort to his young life.

> I am homesick only during the day. I am so homesick now that I don't know what to do. Do not show that to anyone. . . .
>
> I have come from the football. We have won 60 to nothing. If someone doesn't come to see me soon I will die of grief. Please come to see me. I cry sometimes so that I cannot write.
>
> Goodbye dear Papa and Mama
Your little Harry
>
> I have hugged all the pages.

Groton was founded in 1884 by the Reverend Endicott Peabody, an Episcopalian rector and Boston Brahmin whose family motto became "a Peabody or a nobody." His promise to turn his students into "Christian gentlemen" enticed du Ponts, Roosevelts, Harrimans, and other prominent families to entrust their scions to his care. But Peabody's personality ensured that during their tenure the boys would give up some of the amenities to which they were accustomed. The Reverend Peabody's right thinking extended to his decree that all Grotonians be right-handed. Harry was a lefty. He made the change, but his penmanship never recovered. And he had other problems. Until they began receiving the steady, even daily, stream of letters from their son, the du Ponts may not have known of Harry's tenuous grasp of the principles of spelling. Henry Algernon, who wanted his son to excel in all endeavors, was understandably upset: "Remember, the du Ponts are not accustomed to taking a back seat."

To ease Harry's sense of isolation, his parents, sister, grandmother, and many cousins wrote him innumerable letters. His mother's were chatty descriptions of everyday happenings, so detailed that they may have inadvertently made him aware of just how much he was missing. Louise's were affectionate and funny, but they may have rubbed a little salt into the wound since she had not left home. The most remarkable were his father's beautifully written letters, from a time when epistolary form was still a true literary genre. They were a thoughtful continuation of a dialogue that had begun before Harry left Winterthur—"pep talks," practical advice, observations of interest, and most important, the articulation of deeply held beliefs and moral values he wanted to pass on to his son. In response to the revelation that Harry had minimized to his teacher how much French was spoken at home, he penned:

> I write to you this evening, my dear Harry, because I am very much pained to hear of your statement to Mr. Gladwin [Harry's French teacher].
>
> Although I am very glad that you have had the courage to tell your mother and me about it, this is not enough, dear boy. I want you to go to Mr. Gladwin as soon as possible and say to him that the statement you made the other day was not correct and that the fact was that you did usually speak French at home with your mother and me, although you often spoke English with others and habitually with all of your cousins. Finally you must tell Mr. Gladwin that you are very sorry that you did not tell him the exact truth and that you will try not to do so again.

A week later, after receiving a letter from Harry, his father wrote again:

> Among the many cares and anxieties which are continually impressing themselves upon my life, dear Harry, come the disappointment and worry in regard to you.
>
> I have been thinking about your letter all day long and will say in the first place that I am most seriously concerned about your conduct. If you do not behave better you will be sent away from school which would be a terrible misfortune and cause the greatest possible distress to your mother and me! Think of the shame and disgrace, my dear child, and for your own sake and for that of your parents and family as well, keep scrupulously the promises you make in your letter that such bad behavior will not again occur.
>
> Keep constantly in mind, dear boy, the advice I gave you in regard to always telling the *exact truth*. Unless you do this, regardless of the immediate personal consequences, you cannot obtain the confidence and esteem of those about you. . . .
>
> Goodnight, dear, dear child. I love you most tenderly and devotedly. You must be worthy of the name you bear.

From then on Harry usually received high marks in conduct.

As far as his success in academic subjects, he got the proverbial "A" for effort and showed the beginnings of a charmingly self-deprecating sense of humor. "I must say my writing is terrible" is typical of his self-assessments. Occasionally his studies reminded him

Henry Francis du Pont.
c. 1898.

Harry was one of many
students for whom academic
success was not an accurate
predictor of future accomplishments. His parents continually
urged him to work harder, try
more, and perform better. In
1896 Harry reassured them,
"I am beginning to feel like
studying, and I hope it
will last."

of home. In 1896 he wrote, "Dear Mama, I have discovered Brandywine bulbs in Greys Botany their Latin name is 'Mertensia virginica' or Virginian Cowslip, Lungwort, Blue Bells." For several years he had a garden at Groton and even, despite initial opposition from home, took a job with a Mr. Huebner, a local florist, and helped in the greenhouses. When his schoolmates were ill, Harry bought flowers from Huebner's to cheer them, just as his mother would send flowers to cheer him.

The Groton letters reveal a talent that later served Harry well as a garden designer. He could visualize scenes in minute detail and used that ability to assuage his homesickness. Many letters contain passages similar to "The weather is beautiful today and I can see Winterthur and the flowers and everything almost as well as if I were there. I only wish I could be."

CURRICULUM VITAE

In the summer of 1898 the du Ponts hired a tutor to help their son prepare for the Harvard entrance exams. With this extra help, he managed to enter the university with advanced standing in September 1899, forgoing the usual freshman requirements.

At Harvard Harry followed a liberal arts curriculum leading to a bachelor of arts degree. He socialized and took advantage of the many cultural opportunities available in Boston and also visited his family when he could. In June 1900 his sister, Louise, married the well-connected yachtsman and raconteur Francis Boardman Crowninshield and lived part of the year in nearby Marblehead. Harry's life was moving in a pleasant but perhaps aimless direction. Then, in 1901, when he was twenty-one, two fortuitous incidents occurred that helped set him on the path leading to his future life's work: his first trip to Europe and his reacquaintance with a childhood friend.

In the summer of his second year at Harvard, Harry accompanied his family on a trip to Europe to "take the waters" at Aix-les-Bains. From that year on he went to Europe almost annually to study houses and gardens; on several occasions he made world tours. He had discovered that he liked "to see things." When Harry returned to Boston that autumn, Louise reintroduced him to Marian Coffin, who was enrolled as a "special student" in landscape architecture at Massachusetts Institute of Technology (MIT). Marian's mother, Alice Church Coffin, had been a member of Pauline and Henry Algernon's wedding party.

In 1901 landscape architecture was a new profession even for men. The first recorded use of the term was Frederick Law Olmsted's and Calvert Vaux's signatures on their plan for New York City's Central Park in 1858. Marian was a special student at MIT because women were not yet admitted to the program; for a while she was the only female student among 500 men! Whenever Marian could spare a moment from her studies, she and Harry visited gardens, arboreta, and flower shows together. They could hardly have been better situated; turn-of-the-century Boston was the horticultural showplace of the United States.

Asa Gray, a professor at Harvard, had made Boston the center for the study of botany. He established the herbarium named in his honor and developed Harvard Botanic Garden. In 1872 Charles Sprague Sargent was named first director of the university's Arnold Arboretum, a 220-acre tract in Jamaica Plain. He hired Olmsted as landscape architect, and the two men collaborated on the brilliant synthesis of a didactic plant collection laid out as a romantic American landscape park. The arboretum was part of Boston's "Emerald Necklace," a series of waterside green spaces from the Arborway to Franklin Park. The Massachusetts Horticultural Society was one of the first in the United States, founded in 1829.

By 1901, when Harry and Marian began their visits, Arnold Arboretum already contained an unrivaled collection of native American trees, assembled by Sargent during research for his pioneering survey, *Silva of North America*, published in fourteen volumes between 1891 and 1902. In developing the arboretum, Sargent had also collected European and other exotic species and encouraged plant-hunting expeditions to the Far East. Harry had a good eye for plants and, because of the variety of his family's gardens, could identify many of the specimens growing in Boston, but Marian was the young expert on design.

Marian was a highly motivated student. Her reckless, ne'er-do-well father had abandoned his wife and child and drunk himself into an early grave, leaving them almost penniless. Mrs. Coffin and Marian often lived with various relatives in a genteel but rather unsettled existence. Marian educated herself through wide reading in history and other subjects, but inevitable gaps remain in any autodidact's education. When she applied to MIT, the admissions officer required that she be tutored in mathematics before being given even special status.

When Marian and Harry toured gardens, Marian was intent on absorbing the design ideas that each, large or small, embodied and on memorizing the plants used in each composition. The training she was receiving at MIT was in the tradition of the Ecole des Beaux-Arts, the French national school of fine arts, and emphasized drawing skills and the classical ideals of balance, order, proportion, and harmony. Concepts of spatial organization developed as parts of architectural theory were translated directly to the creation of space outdoors.

If this sounds a bit rigid and formulaic in comparison to the bold, romantic approach of a great artist such as Olmsted, it was. It may be impossible to institutionalize genius or

Marian Cruger Coffin. c. 1904.

Coffin's success as a landscape architect was attributable to talent, business acumen, discretion, and fierce determination. As she explained: "A woman has to solve many problems and learn the ropes entirely by herself, while a man has the advantage of long office training and experience." In addition to her work at Winterthur, she designed fifty of the best estate gardens on the East Coast and those of several campuses, including the University of Delaware. Coffin claimed that in order to thrive, a garden needed "money, manure, and maintenance." Fortunately, her friend Harry was quite willing to provide all three for the gardens they designed at Winterthur.

teach creativity, but these first American landscape architecture programs provided a firm grounding in the basic tenets of design. The talent of individual students and the budgets of their clients would determine whether their projects would rise above the ordinary. The record shows that a great many classically inspired, orderly, proportional, and harmonious gardens were designed in America between 1890 and 1930.

One of the courses Harry had completed at Harvard was art history, so he was familiar with most of the terms Marian was, in all likelihood, tossing around, although he may not have heard them used in relation to gardens. In her letters to him, Marian sometimes discussed such things as focal point, forced perspective, and architectural features. Harry's letters were filled with plant names and descriptions. He later demonstrated an innate grasp of design principles but rarely verbalized his understanding or mentioned design theories in his letters, diaries, or notebooks. He certainly appreciated the well-executed flight of steps and gazebo perfectly in scale with its surroundings that Marian designed for him in 1928, but trees, flowers, color, mood, space, atmosphere, and natural form had more emotional resonance.

This is not to say that Marian's approach was all form and Harry's all feeling, but that certainly describes their natural tendencies and the reason they became ideal collaborators many years later. From the beginning of their friendship they identified Marian as the landscape architect and Harry as the plantsman. Especially in their early efforts, he tended to defer to her on questions of architectural design; she sought his advice on plant selection.

The friendship flourished. But there was a disparity—on the one hand, Harry du Pont, a horticultural dilettante born with a silver trowel in his hand, and on the other, Marian Coffin, an individualist striving to overcome economic hardship and the gender bias pandemic in her time in order to reach her professional goals.

Harry made a decision that brought the relationship into balance. Late in October 1901 he sent a letter of application to Bussey Institution, Harvard's college of practical agriculture and horticulture. The school and the adjacent Arnold Arboretum were sited on a 394-acre tract that was a bequest from manufacturer and farmer Benjamin Bussey. The institution was a training school for "young men who intend to become practical farmers, gardeners, florists, and landscape gardeners; as well as for those who will be called upon to manage large estates." In other words, it was for those who might work at places like Winterthur rather than own them. Although Harry's application came after the term had been in session for almost two months, Dean Francis H. Storer relented, "I presume an earnest student could catch up even at this late date by borrowing another student's notes."

Harry's enrolling at Bussey may have struck Henry Algernon as a novel notion, but there is no evidence he opposed the plan. The one near certainty was that Harry would one day own Winterthur. Courses in practical horticulture and a scientific approach to agriculture would be helpful when that day finally arrived. Harry immediately enrolled in Dr. Benjamin M. Watson's Horticulture I and also audited another Watson course, Hardy Herbaceous Plants. On October 29, 1901, he wrote to his mother, "Had my first real lecture in Horticulture today. It was most interesting."

Anyone who has taken that first college-level course in plants can empathize with Harry's predicament in having to memorize fourteen characteristics of 400 plants in a few months: common name, Latin name, family, country of origin, cultural requirements, growth habit, blooming time, flower form, flower color, foliage form, foliage color, possible variations, history of cultivation, and use in design. During spring term he mastered more perennials, ferns, grasses, and water plants. He also learned to prune trees and shrubs. For Propagation, Soils, and Greenhouse Management, students attended laboratories and performed experiments. The lab notebooks they kept reinforced the value of record keeping that Harry had learned from his father.

Bussey's reading lists introduced Harry to two authors whose stars still shine in the horticultural firmament—William Robinson and Gertrude Jekyll. They were both British and both well established, yet their theories and styles had a freshness and verve that proved irresistible to the young man.

Robinson had been born in County Down, Ireland, in 1838. He approached gardening with an almost religious fervor. In *The English Flower Garden* (first published in 1883) he denounced certain late nineteenth-century garden heresies. In the various editions of the book he had chapters on "landscape mistakes near the country house" and "some evils of bedding and carpet gardening." Subtitles continued to reinforce his viewpoint: "Clump Planting Bad," "Dangerous and Ill-placed Trees," "Some Garden Delusions," and so forth. The "bedding-out" he decried was the common practice of raising stridently colored annuals in glasshouses, then using them to "imitate a bad carpet." Robinson thought it was far better to imitate nature, to learn from "the earth itself" about color, form, and placement. He urged his readers to grow the "precious flowers"—native wildflowers and the old-fashioned perennials still seen in cottagers' gardens—and exotics hardy in the English climate. Robinson wrote numerous articles, editorials, essays, and books between 1868 and 1924.

Robinson's friend Gertrude Jekyll was a better writer—the Jane Austen of horticultural literature, with her precise language, innate common sense, and constricted but intense range of vision. She was born in Surrey, England, in 1843. Her aesthetics were closely linked to those of the English Arts and Crafts movement. She was a painter and craftswoman as well as a gardener, until worsening eyesight forced her to paint on the only canvas she could still see—the land. She agreed with Robinson about the value of simple cottage gardens and the lessons to be gleaned from them but suggested, in *Wood and Garden* (1899), that "garden and wooded ground [be treated] in a pictorial way" and that one should "try for beauty and harmony everywhere, and especially for harmony of color." Robinson and Jekyll together are credited with creating what we know as the English flower garden. Jekyll wrote about the American wildflower *Mertensia virginica*, the Virginia bluebells that the du Ponts affectionately called Brandywine bulbs:

> The Sheaf of young leafage comes almost black out of the ground, but as the leaves develop, their dull, lurid colouring changes to a full, pale green of a curious texture, quite smooth, and yet absolutely unreflecting. The dark colouring of the young leaves now only remains as a faint tracery of veining on the backs of the leaves and stalks, and at last dies quite away as the bloom expands. The flower is of a rare and beautiful quality of colour, hard to describe—a rainbow-flower of purple, indigo, full and pale blue, and daintiest lilac, full of infinite variety and indescribable charm.

After reading Jekyll, Harry probably wondered if he had ever really looked at the flower. For a sensitive young gardener, exposure to Jekyll's viewpoint can be a transforming experience.

As Harry pursued his studies, he and Marian exchanged garden books as Christmas presents and continued to visit private gardens such as Holm Lea, Charles Sargent's Brookline estate that he occasionally opened to the public. (Harry met and became friends with Sargent some years later.) Harry took every horticulture-related course he could to complete his degree, including Theory and Principles of Landscape Design. The class studied the great historical garden styles and debated the merits of the formal versus the informal or the architectural versus the naturalistic. The required research paper was an analysis of a landscape design. Harry showed Robinson's influence when he wrote that at the country place he was presenting, boulders were *not* collected and "made into the raised round flower beds planted with the ever prominent red geranium, or some similar constructions ungeological and in shockingly bad taste." Instead, "in the treatment of the grounds everything was done to preserve the original characteristics and natural beauty of the place. . . . The Judas trees and dogwoods were also carefully kept especially along the edge of the woods. . . . The grounds on the north side of the house are entirely wild and no attempt has been made to even clear the undergrowth. There the trees grow in thick profusion among moss covered rocks and wildflowers reign supreme." Harry was analyzing his Aunt Victorine du Pont Foster's Brandywine property, Virieux, but it sounded just like Winterthur.

TRAGEDY AND ITS AFTERMATH

Harry was so pleased with the direction his life had taken that on New Year's Day, 1902, he applied to continue his studies at the School of Practical Agriculture and Horticulture in Briarcliff Manor, New York. The director, George T. Powell, wrote in response, "We take pleasure in having your name head the list for next year, and trust that when the time comes you will be able to join us." Harry left Cambridge for summer vacation with a happy heart. He returned to Winterthur, where things were in a bit of a muddle. His parents were remodeling their house and having their garden redesigned, although it was in essentially the same level spot the Bidermanns had selected many years before. Pauline had been in ill health and decided to visit Louise in Marblehead to get away from the confusion caused by the extensive construction.

Since most of the walls of the home had to be rebuilt, the young horticulturist was frustrated by the inevitable damage to plants growing nearby. He wrote to his mother, "It really would have been much better to have torn the whole thing [the house] down and build a new one as Frank [Crowninshield] suggested this spring." Meanwhile, Harry planted an experimental garden of dahlia varieties and reported the results to his mother, who also loved the cheerful flowers.

Despite her rest, Pauline wasn't getting any better. Until the end of the summer, however, no one could admit how ill she was. On September 20, 1902, Mary Pauline Foster du Pont died of cancer at her daughter and son-in-law's home in Massachusetts. Harry decided to forgo graduate school and remain at Winterthur with his father. It was the best place for Pauline's family to try to heal their broken hearts. Between the many trips back and forth to Marblehead, father and son threw themselves into work. With Harry able to help with the estate, Henry Algernon became increasingly involved in Delaware politics.

Harry had always been interested in all areas of the estate—the farm, the animals, the gardens, and the woods. It was a challenge to apply what he had learned about management and increasing productivity to a real working situation. The new garden spaces were a blessing in disguise. He could plan and plant them without changing his mother's garden and be reminded of their happy times together. In a quirky twist of fate, his mother's death meant that his father needed Harry to manage many of the household details. Without that new responsibility, he might never have noticed that the curtains were changed with the seasons, or cared particularly that the cut-flower production kept pace with the entertaining schedule, or realized how amazed everyone was when the china perfectly matched the flowers on the table. Because he was asked to fill in at a time when he needed a distraction, he brought to domestic matters a youthful energy and previously unsuspected attention to detail. Through the healing power of work and contact with nature, Harry's personal loss effected a change in his perception that would eventually lead to his creation of the most exquisite and complete collection of American decorative arts in the world.

Harry's new responsibilities in the house, farm, and garden required that he keep track of a daunting number of details. He made lists on scraps of paper but soon graduated to notebooks, resuming the habit he had begun at Bussey of always keeping one in his pocket.

He kept notebooks of all sizes on the garden alone. The most important, in terms of his personal aesthetic development and the creation of the garden, contain sequence-of-bloom lists. The first entry, dated February 1, 1902, reads simply, "Scilla." Every day that he could, for the rest of his life, Harry went for a walk at Winterthur and noted what was in bloom. He began recording unusual weather conditions in order to have a more useful comparison from year to year. He took note of the wild trees, shrubs, and flowers, not only the cultivated plants in borders. As his planting schemes grew in complexity, his blooming lists grew in length. By the 1930s he was keeping track of thousands of plants.

The lists were for his own use and did not contain anything that could be called a design theory; however, he often commented on successful plantings, ideas for the future, and maintenance needs. On March 1, 1910, for instance, he noticed the "new daffodil plantation struggling. . . . All leaves should have been removed from Bank to Bend. . . . Do so in future."

In 1910 Harry bought a large, leather-bound garden diary with space on each page for several years' worth of notes, making comparisons even easier. He used this journal until 1959. Only then, when he was seventy-nine, did he officially turn over the task of keeping the list to the professional garden staff. He returned to jotting in a pocket notebook. The garden journals demonstrate Harry's persistence and orderliness, his liking for structured routines, and his use of a scientific approach as a component of artistic decision making. Three overriding concerns or themes emerge from the lists: color, movement, and natural process.

Harry looked very closely at the colors of individual flowers in varying light conditions, in combination with other colors, and as part of the whole landscape. The notebooks are filled with remarks such as that on March 1, 1913: "Mauve crocus fully out—lovely effect with *Narcissus minor*," or on March 27, 1914: "*Scilla bifolia* blue, same color as light shade of *Muscari azureum*." He fell in love with color and its exhilarating possibilities. It was this looking, day after day, year after year, that taught him how color recasts a landscape.

When making his daily census, Harry certainly stopped to smell the flowers, but he was definitely taking a walk. He walked briskly and ranged far beyond the flower borders close to the house. The feeling of movement, the breezes, the changing vistas, the sense of his body in relation to the ancient trees, the chiaroscuro of woods leading to the dazzling openness of the meadow—one can easily imagine all these sensations helping to form his conception of what a garden should be.

He was caught up in nature's rhythms—the yearly cycle of birth, death, and rebirth. Soon he couldn't do without the swelling, budding, bursting, and shriveling that tells us we are a part of something larger than ourselves. Awareness of natural process at first informed, then defined his garden.

PRACTICE MAKES PERFECT

Between 1902 and about 1914 Harry's looking, learning, and listmaking were most intensely concentrated on two large areas—the formal flower garden and his "wild garden."

The flower garden beds were those created during the 1902 house and garden renovation (this page). Photographs and plans indicate a lovely, traditional walled garden with ample opportunities for displaying plants—gates, arbors, pergolas, fountains, and twin garden pavilions (page 80). Four terrace levels included stone paths, lawns, a rectangular water lily pool, and twenty beds for herbaceous borders and a rose garden. It was in those beds that Harry experimented with thousands of plants through the years, trying to perfect his own version of the English flower garden.

He followed Gertrude Jekyll's ideas closely. He collected eight of her books and read many of her articles; there was no dearth of ideas to try. The popular *Colour in the Flower Garden* was published in 1908. Jekyll loved individual plants and wrote persuasively about how a gardener might use each one to best advantage. She advised planting most perennials in graceful "drifts," and Harry did so, developing a method of outlining the shapes with

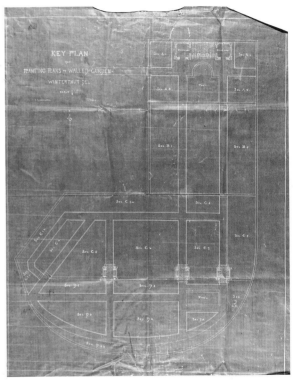

Elizabeth Colwell. Planting plan for walled garden. 1913.

This plan was signed by Elizabeth Colwell, Marian Coffin's assistant, although she was not the designer of the 1902 garden renovation. She copied the original plan in 1913 in order to record various planting schemes of the beds, the site of countless horticultural and artistic experiments.

This autochrome, taken between 1910 and 1916, captures the romantic aura that Harry achieved with herbaceous plants, vines, flowering trees, garden ornaments, water, and architectural features. The peony is a Paeonia suffruticosa *that still grows at Winterthur.*

Opposite: Just as the decorations on a ceramic pot make the surface more visible, the Adonis amurensis *massed on the March Bank help us see it anew. The sunny flowers are especially powerful in contrast to the snow. The bank becomes a yin/yang of quiescence giving way to the promise of new life.*

wires and string that was similar to a technique used by landscape architects to site trees and shrubs but may have been unique in laying out a flower garden. Jekyll suggested varying the height and texture of plants in the border to achieve a dynamic effect, and Harry spent many hours trying to achieve harmony of form. She was one of a very few writers who whole-heartedly presented gardening as a fine art.

Jekyll is justly famous for her writing on color in the garden. Harry often marked those passages that explicated the effect of changing light conditions on the perception of color. Before Jekyll, little had been written in England or America about the use of color in the garden. After her, there was a deluge.

Harry had strong preferences for certain colors and combinations that remained remarkably constant throughout his gardening career. He usually stayed in the cool end of the spectrum, favoring blue, purple, lavender, white, and pink. More often than not he chose pastel tints and shades of his favorite colors. Even when he used yellow, he preferred flowers with a creamy or even greenish tinge. He happily explored all shades of green, the color of nature, as base notes underlying his harmonies and contrasts. As he pointed out in 1962, "Green is one of the prettiest colors there is."

Most of Harry's garden pictures are composed with analogous or related colors, and many areas are playful riffs on shades of the same color. But he also heeded Jekyll's disquisition on the power of complementary color. All through the garden, all through the year, flowers, berries, and leaves whose colors are opposites on the color wheel appear beside each other. In early April, greenish yellow winterhazel blooms with rosy lavender Korean rhododendron. May's spectacular duo is orange-red torch azaleas with soft green ostrich ferns; and in the autumn, lavender beautyberry complements pure yellow *Sternbergia lutea*. The effect is quiet excitement, a punch that doesn't disturb the overall harmony.

Harry tried to duplicate many of Jekyll's ideas and plant combinations exactly. In a notebook on an aster border he wrote, "Follow Miss Jekyll's shape of beds and arrangement of color." Often, however, Delaware's summers, which are hot and humid compared to England's, and occasional bitterly cold winters foiled his efforts.

In a 1910 notebook Harry wrote: "Vine clematis . . . must be tried for a pulled over Jekyll effect behind delphiniums across way." He had more success when he followed her lead in creating a lush, romantic atmosphere with fragrant flowers spilling over paths, vines threading through gnarly old specimen trees or draping languorously over evergreens, and plants weaving through one another, miraculously throwing up flower stalks from every leaf axil. The fact that he couldn't get what he wanted by copying from a book was good for his development as a plantsman and artist. The twenty planting beds were more than a lovely garden; they were Harry's laboratory.

While all the experimenting, reading, buying, growing, watering, pruning, staking, fertilizing, deadheading, evaluating, gnashing of teeth, and pointing with pride was taking place in the flower garden, Harry was also working on a very different project.

In 1870, the same year he visited the United States for the first time, William Robinson published *The Wild Garden*. In subsequent editions, one of which Harry bought soon after college, Robinson tried to clear up any misunderstanding about his title:

> It is applied essentially to the placing of perfectly hardy exotic plants under conditions where they will thrive without further care. It has nothing to do with the old idea of the "Wilderness." . . .What it does mean is best explained by the Winter Aconite flowering under a grove of naked trees in February; by the Snowflake, tall and numerous in meadows by the Thames side; . . . and by the blue Apennine Anemone staining an English wood blue before the coming of our blue bells.

The idea of a wild garden had tremendous appeal for Harry, possibly because he could picture the Winterthur landscape as he read Robinson's words. In 1903 and 1904 he tested 50 varieties of daffodils for suitability for naturalizing. When he had gathered sufficient information, his gardeners planted groups of the best ones in a narcissus grove "on a gentle slope" where the lawn faded into the woods northeast of the house (page 62).

Robinson was not above exaggerating to make a point. He claimed, for instance, that after planting a wild garden, "the owner might go away for ten years and find it more beautiful than ever on his return." The truth behind this horticultural hyperbole is that a wild garden designed to be in tune with nature requires far less maintenance than more formal schemes. In his zeal to cajole people into adopting his methods, Robinson also glossed over the real difficulties of naturalizing bulbs so that they look even remotely natural. Harry came up with a variation on the string-and-wire method he had developed for creating perennial borders. "There is nothing better than a branch to give a charming irregularity of contour and still look natural." His gardeners got into the habit of gathering any fallen branches that happened to have the perfect arch, bend, or crook. They kept these organic templates on hand for whenever du Pont wanted to lay out a naturalistic planting. It wasn't only narcissus but all the so-called minor bulbs and many wildflowers that Robinson prescribed for a wild garden. The area known as the March Bank was directly inspired by his ideas (page 81).

Descendants of daffodils planted long ago in the narcissus grove still appear every year on the March Bank, amid descendants of the scilla and chionodoxa of the wild garden.

Opposite: In April on the bank, the yellow and blue color scheme reasserts itself, now composed of Virginia bluebells and Uvularia grandiflora, *the wildflower called bellwort.*

84

Beginning in 1909 there was a dramatic surge of activity in the garden and grounds at Winterthur. Harry began the major planting on the March Bank, ordering 29,000 bulbs for that and other areas. The bulbs included snowdrops, winter aconite, snowflakes, adonis, squills, glory-of-the-snow, Italian windflowers, Greek windflowers, crocus, iris, grape-hyacinths, miniature daffodils, species tulips, puschkinia, and many others. In 1910 he ordered 39,000 more. It is only because he became ill while traveling in Europe in 1911 and had to rely on his young cousin Anna Robinson to supervise the planting that we have some insight into the complexity of the project.

> I should be very grateful if you would undertake to superintend the planting of these bulbs by Nicholas. All you need to do is walk over the sloping bank looking for wooden labels with names corresponding to those on the list and, in addition, September 1911 written on them. Should there be four or five labels with the same name, what you must do is give the package of those bulbs to Nicholas and say, "Here are the bulbs; they must be divided into two, three, or four lots," as the question may be, and then show him where the places are. I find it is not safe to give him one lot until the one previously given him is planted. After the bulbs are planted I wish you would leave my labels in as they are, simply tying on another wooden label with "Anna" written on it. If, by some mistake, there should not be enough bulbs to fill the required spaces, simply omit planting one of them but kindly mention the fact on a little label. The bank, of course, in addition to the spaces marked is full of labels of bulbs that are already planted there, and naturally these must not be disturbed.

After it was all over, Anna jotted a brief note:

> Dearest Harry—I write in triumph to tell you the bulbs are planted. I have passed sleepless nights at the thought of doing it & now the relief is intense. . . . However, I have decided one thing & that is flowers in their bulbous state are most confusing and that bank is a maze. My admiration for you who evolved it is unbounded.

Every year since, the snowdrops blooming on the March Bank signal spring (pages 84–85). It was in this wild garden that Harry du Pont first stepped beyond the border and saw the whole Winterthur landscape as his garden.

In 1909 Harry was twenty-nine; his father was seventy-one and, as a U.S. senator, lived in Washington, D.C., much of the year. The increased focus on and level of professionalism in garden activities may have resulted from Harry's being given responsibility for the grounds that year.

For the next few years Harry began a great many garden notebooks. These included "Planting Notes—Flower Garden 1909," design and color ideas and plant information; "Gardening Illustrated," articles that interested him in the English weekly periodical; and "Color Schemes, Combinations, Month Gardens." He started two notebooks, one A–M, the other N–Z, categorizing flowers by color. He grouped lists of plants for certain borders by time of bloom, in some cases every two weeks. The borders were blue, blue-yellow, blue-white-yellow, pink, and mauve-purple. One was salmon-coffee! He also kept "Notes on Asters, Annuals, Delphiniums, Irises," "Notes on Peonies, Phlox, Poppies, Roses," "All Other Flowers," "American Gardens and Nurseries," "American Flower Shows," "Changes in Flower Garden," "Permanent Changes in Flower Garden Blueprint," "Bank to Bend," "Notes and Changes to Narcissus Grove and March Bank," and numerous travel notebooks.

In the large hardcover Garden Diary for his sequence-of-bloom lists, Harry began making notes to himself regarding prosaic maintenance needs as well as more artistic concerns: "Alas, alack. . . . Work is behind as Reupke [head of the greenhouse crews] ill for two weeks." In 1910 Harry also commissioned Marian Coffin's assistant, Elizabeth Colwell, to draw up extremely detailed planting plans of the beds in the formal flower garden. He wrote her voluminous letters over the years, specifying each change he made to the borders.

Between 1909 and the outbreak of World War I Harry traveled abroad, especially in England, visiting gardens and horticultural exhibitions. He made two long trips with Marian and her mother in 1909 and 1912. He met Gertrude Jekyll and twice visited her garden at Munstead Wood and also saw the gardens of William Robinson, Ellen Willmott, Sir Frank Crisp, and many of the famous horticulturists of his era.

In 1912 Harry made a list of perennials to be planted, most of which he had ordered on a long trip that year. There were hundreds of species, with separate lists for poppies (16 cultivars), iris (58 cultivars), and verbascum (8 cultivars), along with his comments, "*Veronica spuria* more graceful and not quite as deep a *spicata*." Many of these plants were put in trial beds for evaluation. He also drew up a seven-page list of plant labels to be ordered. A similar, but shorter list was typed for 1913, but these included only herbaceous perennials, not the thousands of bulbs, shrubs, and trees on the estate.

Between 1909 and 1916 a professional photographer documented work in the formal flower garden in black and white images. As soon as the first color process was commercially available, Henry Algernon purchased a camera and glass plates for his son, so that Harry and H. B. McCullom, the du Ponts' assistant, could capture the garden in color.

Autochrome of the white border in the walled garden. c. 1913.

Two French brothers, Auguste and Louis Lumière, invented the autochrome process: glass plates were coated with an emulsion to which dyed potato starch particles could adhere. After processing, the plates became a softly colored positive transparency. The exposure time was so prolonged that if flowers were being photographed, they usually blew in the wind, further enhancing the soft, impressionistic effect.

Harry and McCullom took more than 400 autochromes of the flower garden and the wild garden between 1910 and 1916 (above).

Sometime between 1909 and 1915 the young man of few words decided to write a book, which he thought of titling "A Delaware Garden, with Colored Illustrations." He got as far as the preface, which took the form of an apologia because there were so many worthwhile books already in print. Chief among these were "the very excellent *Garden Month by Month*" by Mabel Cabot Sedgwick and "many volumes by English authors which none who are interested in gardening and horticulture can well afford not to read." But, since in his locality, "it is practically impossible to reproduce satisfactorily the English effects, he is now going to give the benefit of his experiments and trials to any who may be interested."

Although Henry Algernon may have asked his son to manage the garden operations, Winterthur still belonged to the elder man, and Harry sometimes had to finesse inevitable differences of opinion. In the autumn of 1911, for instance, he wrote to John Chapple, who worked in the greenhouses: "Please do not wait too late to have the sash out

Opposite: Daffodils above the Quarry Garden.

If Harry had written a book about gardening, he probably would have included the advice he gave in The Daffodil and Tulip Year Book 1961: *"Always plant the varieties separately. This is one of the essential and all-important lessons the intending planter must learn, as there can be no comparison as to the more pleasing effect of a bold expanse of one variety than that of a mixture."*

of the conservatory. I know the Colonel [Henry Algernon] likes it to be uncovered as long as possible, but he sometimes does not realize the length of time it takes to put it up, and I do not want to take any risk of having the plants frozen." Harry and his father usually worked together. One such instance involved the collection of conifers known as the Pinetum. After Henry Algernon lost his Senate seat in 1917, horticulture became the consuming interest of his last years. As Harry worked on major plantings along the Winterhazel Walk and in Azalea Woods, Henry Algernon added trees and shrubs to the landscaping closer to the house, as he had when he first brought Pauline to Winterthur almost fifty years before.

Each year Harry assumed more responsibilities at Winterthur and in the wider community. No matter how busy he became, however, he always thought of the garden, walked in the garden, read about gardening, and bought plants for the garden. There was only one year when less work was accomplished. In 1916 Harry married the beautiful Ruth Wales (this page). Regardless of how enticing the distractions, some habits of mind are hard to change. A letter to his father that Harry composed while he and Ruth were on their honeymoon trip to British Columbia reads in part, "The pure yellow dogtooth violets are enchanting and I am sending Reupke a lot of seeds."

Postscript

DEAREST KID

Among his circle of lifelong friends, Harry's sister, Louise, held a special place. Their frequent letters, full of colorful detail about family and friends, reveal a singular degree of sibling warmth and affection as well as their rather striking similarities of talents and interests. At the time of Harry's engagement to Ruth Wales, Louise wrote:

> Tuesday
>
> Dearest Kid [a salutation much used during Harry's Groton days],
>
> I was so stunned (though I was sure on Sat and Sun) by the great news that I have not recovered my breath yet and could not tell flowers from weeds all day with most dire results. There are so many things I wanted to talk about; you were cruel not to tell me all that way to Aunt Lina's. I hoped every minute you would. After 36 years you really do not know me much. I never tell important things [that I am not supposed to].
>
> Do write me a few details. June 1st is so far away and you will be so busy then. I feel too far off and out of it—but oh dear boy—I am so glad, so really glad, that this happiness should have come to you—and you know—I have always thought Ruth a sweetie and so intelligent and bright and just "the person."
>
> Lots and lots of love,
> Yours ever,
> L.

Ruth Wales du Pont. June 24, 1916.

After her marriage, Ruth Wales du Pont studied music at the Peabody Institute in Baltimore. One of her compositions, Fugue in G Minor, was recorded in 1993 by the New Tankopanicum Orchestra (Brian Cox, conductor) on the compact disc Music from the Banks of the Brandywine.

NATURE INTO ART

Denise Magnani

He had to choose. But it was not a choice.
Between excluding things. It was not a choice

Between, but of. He chose to include the things
That in each other are included, the whole,
The complicate, the amassing harmony.
Wallace Stevens, "Notes Toward a Supreme Fiction" 1942

I came back fired with the desire to plant azaleas in all directions.
H. F. du Pont 1930

If Azalea Woods were a painting, the artist would be Claude Monet. The title of this landscape painting might have something to do with flowers, but its subject would be a fleeting moment captured by brush strokes of shimmering, color-filled light (opposite).

Azalea Woods is not a painting, but it is a work of art. Every spring for forty years Harry du Pont returned to the woods, checking to see if his celebration of color was in need of a touch-up. Just as Impressionism remains the most beloved of modern artistic movements, Azalea Woods is by far the most popular of all the plantings at Winterthur.

Some critics argue that people tend to like the Impressionists for the wrong reasons —for the prettiness of their pictures—when the artists felt themselves to be intent explorers of color, light, and perception. Harry labored at his craft as fervently as any painter ever did. But when the crowds lined up for his "changing exhibition" in May, he was just happy they knew what they liked.

It cannot be denied: Azalea Woods is incredibly pretty. Beneath the great canopy of trees whose spring green leaves are still unfurling, the understory of white flowering dog-

The merest breath of air causes the Italian windflower petals to vibrate, or so it seems. The arrangement of petals—thin, straplike, skyward facing—and color range—from white through palest sky blue, sometimes with a hint of lavender—create an impression of flickering in the spring light.

wood blooms with carefully modulated waves of pastel color from hundreds of azaleas. On the forest floor, a gorgeous tapestry is woven with great white trilliums, Italian windflowers, and Spanish bluebells. Every tree, shrub, and wildflower seems to be in improbable full bloom at once. The *succession* of blooming is far more complex, with some species flowering in early April and the last blossom opening by mid June. It is May, however, when garden visitors feel surrounded by lyrical color, as if in the midst of a painting.

The colors for this landscape were "made in Japan." Most of the azaleas in the 8-acre Azalea Woods are Japanese Kurume hybrids. Harry chose azaleas in predominantly pastel shades. He grouped and regrouped them in patterns to illustrate the relationships among cognate colors. He employed vivid and striking colors more sparingly, often juxtaposing them with contrasting shades that intensified one another's effect. In all his combinations he demonstrated how context determines perception.

An analysis of his floral configurations reveals two painterly techniques: compositional unity achieved through repetition of color (both spatially and temporally) and variety within an apparently unified and monochromatic color scheme by the introduction of subtlety and nuance.

What appears at first glance to be a large planting of the same white Kurume azalea is actually three different cultivars: 'Snow,' a pure-white hose-in-hose (a flower with a double corolla); #16, a single (one row of petals) greenish white blossom; and 'Rose Greeley,' a semidouble white. In botanical Latin there are twenty separate words for degrees or qualities of whiteness; Harry was not alone in appreciating minute differences (page 96).

Another bed in the woods is composed of *R. kurume* #6, a single, white-striped mauve azalea, and 'Cattleya,' a white hose-in-hose with a mauve edge. Yet another group has *R. kurume* #46, a single flower in salmon pink with a blush of white; #47, an irregular hose-in-hose in the white and salmon pink of #46; and #48, the same salmon pink in a solid color. Harry assigned numbers to the unnamed Kurumes to correspond with their blooming time. The artist is surely having fun with us, rewarding us for peering into the soul of a flower. Just as surely and deftly, he is showing us what he has learned about color in the woods.

Harry always used certain azaleas in combination. His favorite pink triad was the famous hose-in-hose 'Pink Pearl,' the lighter pink hose-in-hose 'Appleblossom'—these two are such a close color match that the difference is apparent only upon close scrutiny—and *R. kurume* #10, a double rose pink blossom that is clearly darker than the others (pages 98–99). He created white/pink/salmon combinations, white-striped mauve groups, and shades of lavender, white, and salmon/red plantings. The 8 acres seem to contain an endless variety of azaleas. There are, in fact, only about twenty different kinds, with at least twenty-five plants of each chosen cultivar in the large beds, arranged in artful combinations to expatiate on the theme of harmonious color.

In his exploration of color Harry discovered something that the Impressionists knew, as do all painters and photographers who work outdoors: intense natural light bleaches color. Light that reaches the forest floor, however, is diffused and fractured during its journey through the leafy canopy. For the artist who gardens in the woods, the palest colors are luminous beacons that draw us into the depths of the forest.

INTO THE WOODS

A painting can be about the insubstantial—light, color, mood—but a garden must exist in at least three dimensions. Harry didn't begin Azalea Woods on a blank canvas but within the entity known as the eastern deciduous forest.

Forests have an architectural structure that typically is thought to consist of four layers. The tallest trees form the canopy, and understory trees are smaller species that have adapted to the light that filters through the leafy crown. The next layer is made of shrubs able to survive in even less light, and below them are woodland wildflowers, ferns, and mosses. The particular mix of species is determined by many factors, including climate, soil structure and composition, and stage of woody succession, or age of the forest.

The woods that Harry played in as a child were second-growth oak-chestnut forests, the principal mesic forest of the piedmont area of rolling countryside east of the Appalachians. American chestnuts; white, red, and black oaks; the quickly growing tulip-poplars; white ash; red maples; and various hickories were abundant in the canopy. Another woodland giant, the distinctive silver-gray barked American beech often grew in clusters, usually on north-facing slopes.

Along the Brandywine the woods are chilly, dank, and silent through the winter. In late February there are faint stirrings; by April the woods are throbbing with life, both floral and faunal. As Brandywine naturalist and landscape architect Ted Browning wrote:

> What really enables mid-April plants to flash so explosively in our minds and across the landscape is simply that there are no leaves on the trees to obscure them, to tone them down, to melt them away into foliage. Mid-April flowers sparkle across a brown-hued, green-tinted landscape in the same way that the colors of a rising trout sparkle in the green-brown depths of a stream. . . . Spring ephemerals—woodland

plants that grow, leaf, flower and fade in the strong light before the forest trees leaf out—dot the forest floor with spots of color and scent. Hepatica in blue, white, and pink. Trout-lily in yellow. Toothwort in white. Dutchman's breeches in white tinged with a bit of yellow. Spring beauty in white tinged with a bit of pink.

The understory trees and shrub layer also come alive in spring. In late March yellow puffballs decorate the black-twigged spicebush; by mid April lovely pale pink covers the wild azalea called pinxterbloom. Perhaps the most beautiful of all is the white or pink flowering dogwood at the woodland's edge in May.

The eastern forest is a community of many interdependent plants and animals, each species with its own cycle of decay and regeneration. The forest as a whole is a complex and fragile web of life. In 1904 a fungus disease from the Far East began to ravage American chestnuts all along the eastern seaboard. The rapidly spreading chestnut blight was the worst ecological disaster of the era and within fifty years all but eliminated the stately native from the canopy. If the demise of the American chestnut hadn't broken a strand in the web, Harry would probably never have begun the painstaking, ultimately joyful process of forest abstraction —the deletion of the extraneous and the addition of the meaningful—that turned nature into art.

SELVA OSCURA

When the chestnut blight reached the woods at Winterthur, both Harry and his father were devastated. The only known method of halting the spread of the insect-borne disease was to remove infected trees. By about 1912 many had been cut, hauled from the estate's various wooded tracts, and burned, leaving huge gaps in the canopy and on the forest floor. About this time the du Ponts became acquainted with the world's foremost authority on North American trees, Charles Sprague Sargent, director of the Arnold Arboretum in Massachusetts.

Harry was just the sort of person Sargent liked—someone who was deeply interested in plants and committed to the advancement of American horticulture and who had some disposable income that might be donated to the never-full coffers of the arboretum. Once they connected, the two men formed a relationship that was both pleasant and mutually rewarding. Harry became a donor to and lifelong advocate of Arnold Arboretum and was the recipient of numerous plants that were introduced into cultivation under the arboretum's aegis. In 1917 Sargent asked him to serve as a member of the Harvard Board of Overseers' Committee to Visit the Arnold Arboretum:

Above: Some say the great white trillium is our most beautiful native wildflower. Both its deep green leaves and pure white petals come in three parts. The white is so bright that one common name for the flower is snow trillium—a fitting groundcover beneath the double azalea 'Snow.' This use of double and triple whiteness was Harry's way of increasing the viewer's awareness without calling undue attention to the means.

Below: The mood is one of serenity. The viewer is wrapped in, and enraptured by, pastel harmonies. But things are not just what they seem. There are fewer different varieties of azaleas than imagined but more differences among the flowers than can be believed. The arrangement addresses our human responsibility for understanding our world, our capacity for taking pleasure in this beauty.

Azaleas 'Pink Pearl,'
'Appleblossom,' and
R. kurume #10.
Look closely. Enjoy.

Inset: The layered structure of
the northeastern forest is cele-
brated in the garden. Harry's
aesthetics were rooted in the
reality of his daily existence. He
worked from solid information,
not to redo the world but to
reframe it slightly, just enough
to highlight something of
significance.

The committee appointed by the Overseers has been of very great service to me now for many years in aiding [and] . . . in raising enough money . . . to keep the establishment going, the income from the endowment being entirely inadequate for that purpose. While the Committee has been of great service to the Arboretum in this way I have never gotten any horticultural or other advice from its members, and when I suggested to the Overseers to appoint you a member of the Committee it was with the idea that you should be able to help me horticulturally for in this direction I am left entirely without advice or assistance.

With the exception of the academic years 1923/24 and 1966/67, Harry served on the board until 1968.

An even closer friendship flourished between Harry's father and Sargent, who were nearly the same age and possessed similar temperaments and worldviews. Their association, which lasted from about 1917 until Henry Algernon's death in 1926, had an enormous influence on the plant collection at Winterthur. When Sargent learned in 1918 that Henry Algernon had begun to plant evergreens, he wrote:

I am very much interested in a Pinetum in Delaware and I hope that you will favor the plan of establishing one there on your place. Except in the neighborhood of Boston and on Long Island there is no good collection of conifers anywhere in the United States, and one is needed in your region where probably many species can be grown which are not hardy here or near New York. I enclose a rough list of conifers which can probably all be successfully grown on your place and which I do not remember to have seen there. Some of these are not difficult to obtain but others probably are not now to be found in nurseries. Sooner or later, however, we can get them all together for you, I feel sure, if you will undertake this patriotic work.

Many of the rarest of the fifty or so species and varieties in the Pinetum came directly from Sargent between 1918 and 1925. In 1919 he sent Henry Algernon some of the flame-red torch azaleas (*Rhododendron kaempferi*), a species Sargent himself collected in Japan. Henry Algernon joined his son in making regular contributions to the Arnold Arboretum to support Sargent's work.

The last letter Henry Algernon wrote to Sargent contains these lines: "Although it is said that really deep and lasting friendships must have their origin in the affiliations of boy-hood or youth I must say that while our relations only began long subsequent to this, I have no friend now living in whom my interest is more cordial and profound." The two men died within three months of each other, du Pont on the last day of 1926 and Sargent on March 22, 1927.

Most of the plants sent to Winterthur from the Arnold Arboretum during Sargent's directorship and later were originally found in Asia. There had been a continuous wave of Western botanists scouring the Japanese landscape for plants since 1858, when Japan reluctantly signed a limited trade treaty with the United States. Before that, missionaries, scientists, and explorers (Marco Polo among them) had brought back seeds and samples of an extensive Far Eastern flora. All the samples collected between 1853 and 1856 by the United States Surveying Expedition to the North Pacific Ocean ended up in Boston on the desk of Asa Gray, professor of botany at Harvard.

Gray had heard and read reports of the great diversity of species from China and Japan and put aside other projects to examine the expedition's findings. Many of the specimens were eerily similar and, in some cases, exactly like plants native to eastern North America. To account for the morphological similarities of plants from the two physically separated areas as well as the fact that no such similarities occurred in the flora of intervening geographic regions, Gray formulated an elegant hypothesis based on a common origin for the two groups in preglacial epochs. That theory is summarized in *A Reunion of Trees* (1990) by Stephen A. Spongberg, the present horticultural taxonomist with the Arnold Arboretum:

> Before the glacial epoch the flora of the North Temperate Zone had been relatively homogeneous, extending in a more or less undisrupted belt across North America and Eurasia. During the Pleistocene, when the glaciers began their advance southward from the polar region, great areas . . . became covered by glacial ice . . . [and] the temperate flora migrated southward—where that was possible. . . . In areas where barriers prevented southward migration, the flora was severely decimated or was completely destroyed as the climatic conditions deteriorated. . . . In much of western North America and Eurasia the climate was sufficiently altered by a series of other geologic phenomena—mountain building in particular—that the old temperate flora could not reclaim its former territory without drastic adaptation through evolution. In these regions new species evolved to replace the preglacial, or Arctotertiary species became discontinuous in the postglacial world. In eastern North America and eastern Asia, the old Arctotertiary flora had either escaped the vicissitudes of the Pleistocene or was able to reclaim its former territory without drastic adaptation. Thus, the similar floras in the two regions today constitute relics of the preglacial flora that once encircled the globe.

In all, 120 genera of plants were found showing this same pattern of distribution. In the northern hemisphere, eastern Asia was the place where, by far, the greatest number of

Overleaf left: The vaulted canopy becomes a cathedral, a holy place for contemplation, even revelation. Leaving, one is not quite the same person as when one enters. Gardeners have always sought paradise; Harry found his in Azalea Woods.

Overleaf right: Beneath tulip-poplars, torch azaleas from Japan light up the woods. Woodland phlox, buttercups, mayapples, English bluebells— these are the plants in the great American garden.

species successfully recolonized the postglacial landscape, with eastern North America second. Gray published his thesis in 1859, the same year his friend Charles Darwin's *Origin of Species* appeared. In postulating a common ancestry for Asian and North American plants, Gray was providing evidence in support of evolution through natural selection.

As fascinating as all of this was from a scientific standpoint, the practical consequence for American gardeners was the probability that they could grow the Asian counterparts of North American dogwoods, witch-hazels, cherries, and rhododendrons in their gardens.

As early as 1907, Cottage Gardens Companies of Long Island began importing directly from Yokohama Nursery Company in Japan. Cottage Gardens, directed by Robert T. Brown, was one of Harry's favorites. On one visit to the nursery, he spied seventeen compact azaleas covered with small glossy leaves but no flowers. Brown had purchased them after Yokohama won a gold medal for showing fifty-two varieties at the Panama-Pacific Pacific Exposition in San Francisco in 1915. They were called Kurume hybrid azaleas after the city on the Japanese island of Kyushu, where Motozo Sakamoto originally bred wild forms in 1820. Harry purchased all seventeen plants.

PARADISE REGAINED

Back at Winterthur Harry made the step in the design process that is facetiously known among landscape architects as the GCL: Great Creative Leap. He asked his gardeners to plant the Kurume azaleas in the woods so recently decimated by the removal of the American chestnuts. The following May, 1918, he discovered that the plants were not only hardy but were covered with blossoms in his favorite colors. His own version of the development of Azalea Woods doesn't give too much away: "I told Mr. Brown I would take these seventeen plants and practically all the Kurumes I have naturalized in our woods are cuttings from them. The Chestnut Blight had left many openings, and before I knew it Robertson, our Scottish gardener, had numerous young Kurume plants with no place to go except the woods, where they have been ever since" (page 103).

Each year gardeners grew more Kurumes for Harry to work into the woods. He composed his color schemes *en plein air* as the Impressionists had done a generation before. Each May he carried flowering sprigs, in Winterthur Dairy milk bottles, from plant to plant to compare hues, shades, and tints in the dappled light of the spring woodland. He made decisions on the spot, and a crew dug and moved azaleas in full bloom so he could evaluate the changes immediately. This process continued for years. According to one gardener, some of the plants "were in five or six holes."

Not only azaleas were on the move. Harry kept several arborists busy from morning to night, judiciously pruning the great trees to allow more light to reach the shrub layer. Gardeners added hundreds of flowering dogwood to those already growing naturally at the woodland edge—*Cornus florida* blooms with Kurume azaleas. They planted showy Chinese and Japanese viburnums near wild ones to extend the flowering season. Thousands of Spanish bluebells followed thousands of Virginia bluebells. All layers of the woods were there, but Harry brought them to his idea of perfection. If he had to get his shrub layer from halfway around the world, so be it.

It was the shrub layer of azaleas that simultaneously extended Harry's vocabulary of form and broadened his color palette. An evergreen Asian azalea in full bloom provides the artist with color that has a solidity and heft impossible to achieve with herbaceous perennials alone (even when they are used in staggering numbers, as on the March Bank). A significant artistic breakthrough in the making of Azalea Woods was Harry's realization that he could use shrubs and small flowering trees to compose naturalistic garden spaces and satisfy his intense longing for ubiquitous color.

Eventually Azalea Woods grew to 8 acres, limited only by the fields and golf course at the outer edges of the woodland patch where Harry started his experiment. After the enlargement in 1945, he sent a note to Marian Coffin: "The azalea plantation is on its way, and I am delighted and feel that I can be gathered to my Father with a calm sense of repose."

Harry religiously followed the work carried out by plant breeders using Asian azaleas, and if their results enhanced his color schemes or blooming sequences, the new azaleas became part of the Winterthur garden. Du Pont contacted Charles O. Dexter after learning of his pioneering work in breeding large-leaf evergreen Asian rhododendrons for hardiness. Soon a truck laden with flats of unnamed rhododendron hybrid seedlings was delivered to Winterthur. When they reached flowering size in test plots, Harry used the best in Azalea Woods to provide architectural structure at midlevel and a final surge of color and fragrance in late May and early June (page 102).

A most intriguing historical footnote to the story of Azalea Woods has remained untold because of du Pont's inherent modesty. The official date for the establishment of Azalea Woods is 1918, when the first seventeen Kurumes from Cottage Gardens bloomed. On March 10, 1920, Charles Sargent wrote Harry:

> Two weeks from today, March 24th, there is to be a flower show in Boston lasting through the following Sunday. One of the features will be a collection of the new race of Azaleas which Wilson brought back from Japan and which have not been

seen before in the eastern United States or in Europe. . . . I think you ought to come and see them, especially as we have every reason to hope that this race of Azaleas will prove hardy in Wilmington, I am afraid that the climate of Massachusetts will be too severe for them. The flowers are beginning to open and there are delightful colors among them. If these Azaleas prove hardy in the middle states they will be the most important introduction to the gardens of that part of the country which has been made for a great many years.

The Wilson to whom Sargent referred was Ernest H. Wilson, assistant director of the Arnold Arboretum, who was nicknamed "Chinese" because of his astonishing success in discovering garden-worthy plants in China and Japan. He and Sargent were especially excited about Kurume azaleas and tirelessly promoted them in the early 1920s. In one of his many books, *Plant Hunting* (1927), the ebullient Wilson introduced the "Princess Kurume" to the American gardener. Not wanting to steal anyone's thunder, du Pont never mentioned that he had been growing Kurumes at Winterthur since 1917.

Every landscape has a story to tell those who listen. Azalea Woods speaks of the beauty of the piedmont forest, the triumph over adversity, of expanding knowledge and a shrinking globe, of creativity, and the humanized landscape (below). It reveals almost everything we want to know about azaleas. In 1961 du Pont prepared an article in which he noted:

Rhododendron kaempferi was collected in Japan by Charles Sprague Sargent and sent soon after to Winterthur. It is called the torch azalea for its fiery color and upright shape. The sturdy ostrich ferns grow to 4 feet. Together at one of the entrances to Azalea Woods, they are a perfect contrast in color, an apt complement in form.

The longer I grow the azaleas the more I realize how beautiful they are when grouped in harmonious colors and pleasing contrast. They naturalize in every imaginable terrain and contour (no other species are in bloom in Delaware for almost four months) and due to their various heights and habits of growth they are never monotonous and are perfect with countless varieties of bulbs and wild bloom.

As he had done in the past and would do in the future, Harry underplayed his hand. He wrote almost as if azaleas, not he, created the garden. They were so beautiful that he had to make his garden in the woods. Harry fell in love with Princess Kurume, and Winterthur was never the same.

Postscript
GRACE NOTES

Henry Francis du Pont liked to make efficient use of every minute, yet he had time for the niceties of life, among them the thoughtful gesture. Years after he had happened on the Kurume azaleas that form the core of Azalea Woods, he wrote to Robert T. Brown, the owner of Cottage Gardens Nursery:

> I shall always be grateful to you for those Kurume Azaleas you sold me years ago, and I should like you to come down and see them and their children and grandchildren. I imagine they will be in bloom between May 11th and 16th.

Despite failing health, Brown made the trip to Winterthur that spring. After his visit he wrote:

> I want to tell you how much I enjoyed my visit with you going over the Azaleas. The display was such a marvelous one that I will never forget it and I wish now to thank you very much for the opportunity of seeing them.

At this time (1962) Silvia Saunders, daughter of the preeminent peony hybridizer A. Percy Saunders, was getting "some small inkling" of the complexity of Harry's life. She, with help and encouragement from Harry, was about to mount an exhibit of her father's peonies for the Royal Horticultural Society's Chelsea Show—transporting some 400 blossoms from Winterthur to London, where their display was awarded the Lindley Silver Medal.

> Harry, this expedition . . . is giving me a sense of what your life is Everyday and All Day. I am more and more astounded at all that you do . . . and the heart behind it. My gratitude and wonder are very very deep.

AN ARRANGED MARRIAGE

Robert F. Trent and Denise Magnani

Garden and building may now be one.

FRANK LLOYD WRIGHT, *AN ORGANIC ARCHITECTURE* 1939

Although the house [Virieux] if placed elsewhere would look
somewhat tall and boxlike, yet as it is now with high trees
on two sides of it, it fits in with its surroundings
and together with the grounds impresses one
with a sense of tranquility and beauty.

H. F. DU PONT 1903

Henry Francis du Pont, who had been collecting American decorative arts since 1923, inherited Winterthur early in 1927. "Within a year," writes Jay E. Cantor in *Winterthur* (1985), "he had woodwork from Chestertown and Centreville, Maryland; he had rooms from Tappahannock, in Virginia; from the Pickering House in North East, Maryland; and Belle Isle in storage and had measured drawings of these rooms on hand." H. F. du Pont intended to add his own American wing to the family residence to display his ever-growing collection. On May 3, 1928, he asked Wilmington architect Albert Ely Ives to begin plans. A few weeks later, du Pont offered Marian Coffin the job of redesigning the landscape.

> Dear Marian,
>
> I am thinking of putting an addition to this house and changing the front door to an entirely different place, which means re-arranging the grounds at the back of the house towards the garden entirely.
>
> I am sending you a blueprint showing the present location of the wall near the house here, and the walk to the garden. I shall roughly plot on this plan the pro-posed location of the new wing. I thought we had better build a retaining wall on

A postconstruction view of the grand staircase to the east of the 1928–31 addition demonstrates how it was almost on axis with du Pont's bedroom window (barely visible at the head of the stairs). The cross axis at the landing leads to the 1902 plant-ing beds that Coffin worked into her redesign.

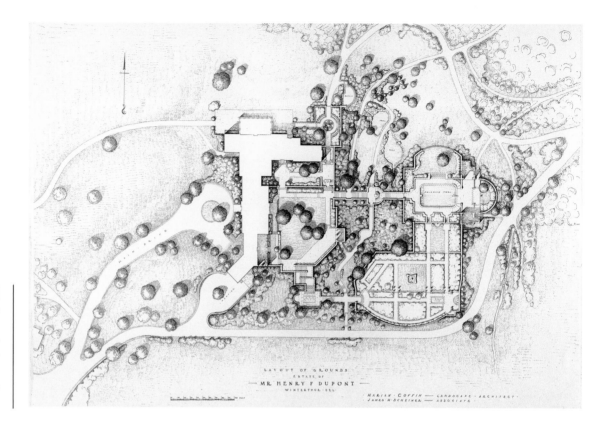

The final planting plan by Marian Coffin for H. F. du Pont's landscape surrounding the 1928–31 wing is the best proof that du Pont had a vision for integrating his house and garden.

the lower part of the lawn and make a flat terraced garden below the group of poplar trees and one beech tree shown on the plan. I have a great number of figures, benches, wall fountains, etc., collected over a period of years, which I thought could be used to advantage here. The center of this garden would be on axe [axis] with the steps leading to the new open terrace which I think of using outside my dining room.

For the front entrance forecourt, I have taken the same size as we had in Southampton. . . . I will want the garden to be finished with the house, so I would like to have immediate concentration of thought upon it.

Marian immediately tended to her old friend's request. Two years earlier she had designed the landscape at Chestertown House, du Pont's home in Southampton, New York. The commission at Winterthur she now undertook was to be the largest of her career.

As always, du Pont did not want to obliterate the past but rather use it as a starting point. Although he was going to build a new wing—the largest single addition made before or since to the main house at Winterthur—he had a great deal of regard for the existing garden. In a second letter to Marian dated twelve days later, Harry reiterated his desire to "not interfere with the slope and the fine poplar and beech trees." Preserving other features, like a garden gate and a wisteria vine, is also mentioned in the letter.

The plan Marian drafted by that autumn demonstrates how skillfully she worked with her client to fit the new structure and garden fixtures into the existing landscape (opposite). The addition to the house was in many ways extremely daring because it went directly south, downhill, creating a building that eventually totaled nine stories. Du Pont mentioned the idea of merging the large addition with the landforms in his original letter to Ives, but never gave his rationale. One reason certainly was his wish to save as many trees as possible. Another may have been that he was looking forward to a prolonged campaign of installing period rooms in this new wing. By extending the house outward and down the hill, he provided for himself a narrow, high structure with many windows; he could install rooms at liberty and still be sure of adequate light and access as well as views of the surrounding landscape (below).

Clearly visible in the center of Coffin's plan is the blank space representing the house with its new extension. To the west of the wing is a circular drive exactly the same size as the forecourt Coffin had designed a few years earlier at Chestertown. The drive leading up to the turnaround meanders through a grove of tulip-poplars whose immense size is not apparent from the plan. At first glance, Coffin's roads appear to be deceptively simple. The driveway leads up to the house, while a subsidiary road much farther down the hill leads to a similar turnaround that functions as a service entrance. Further inspection reveals that a new bridge and slight bend in the entry drive subtly present the new wing to an approaching visitor. The gently curving paths and terrace levels on the west side of the wing (not shown on the plan) provide successful circulation routes and opportunities for planting.

The north end of the building plan reinforces how great a departure du Pont's extension to the south was. A long, rather informal series of extensions had already been added to either side of the original (1837–39) Winterthur building in 1874, 1884, and 1902. The small protruding square at the north end of the new plan, with a somewhat broken outline, is a new glass-walled conservatory. This west-to-east complex was essentially what du Pont had inherited from his father early in 1927.

This view of the extreme southern end of the wing during construction shows how the building was placed between trees that were carefully preserved as part of the garden design.

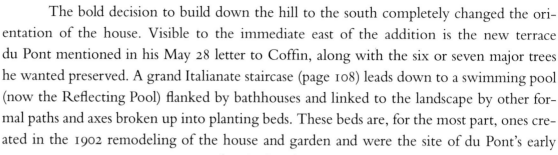

The bold decision to build down the hill to the south completely changed the orientation of the house. Visible to the immediate east of the addition is the new terrace du Pont mentioned in his May 28 letter to Coffin, along with the six or seven major trees he wanted preserved. A grand Italianate staircase (page 108) leads down to a swimming pool (now the Reflecting Pool) flanked by bathhouses and linked to the landscape by other formal paths and axes broken up into planting beds. These beds are, for the most part, ones created in the 1902 remodeling of the house and garden and were the site of du Pont's early horticultural experimentation.

Views of the Iris Garden and Latimeria Summerhouse on the extreme west of the planting plan. c. 1930.

It isn't clear from the plan why the entryway on the west side was not on line with the grand staircase leading down the hill to the east. Once more, existing trees seem to have played a part in the decision. It cannot have been entirely a coincidence that when du Pont established his living quarters on the seventh floor of the new wing, his bedroom was almost exactly on axis with the great Italianate staircase. The dates of the architect's and landscape architect's plans indicate that he intended a relationship between the interior of the new addition and the landscape. Before du Pont had much of an opportunity to build many of the period rooms in his addition, he had already substantially planned and constructed the garden context for the building. It follows that he calculated vistas and color schemes that complemented the existing exterior landscape.

The result of the collaboration between du Pont and Coffin appears effortless today. Their garden, however, embodies a delicate balance struck between two divergent, almost opposed, approaches to the creation of landscape. Throughout her career, Coffin remained true to the design philosophy she absorbed at MIT. Her friend Warren Hunting Smith wrote: "She regarded axial design as essential even in the most informal gardens." Du Pont's style, in contrast, became increasingly subtle and naturalistic with each passing year. Little of the axial design and ornate masonry associated with Italian and French gardens appears at Winterthur today, especially farther from the main building and the formal terraces and beds around it. Du Pont and Coffin were able to bring their artistic impulses into harmony despite their difference in approach because he insisted on being involved with every step in the process and she respected both his horticultural expertise and his concept of the garden as part of the natural surroundings—in this case, the northeastern forest and the enclosing agricultural landscape. Besides, he was paying the bills.

Coffin developed several informal gardens away from the main house at the same time that she designed its Italianate terraces. Northwest of the swimming pool she created a series of pools and waterfalls (now called the Glade Garden) crafted of 100 tons of imported limestone, among which du Pont placed alpine plants and wildflowers. To the west of the new wing, off to the side of the main drive, Coffin designed an iris garden (opposite above). (Because the iris hybrids were subject to disease, the area was later replanted as a peony garden.) She incorporated in this configuration a sunken terrace and a long path leading toward Azalea Woods. This path is anchored at the south end by a small summerhouse that Harry had salvaged from Latimeria (opposite below), the Wilmington estate of Mary Latimer. At the north end a latticework open doorway, marking the end of the vista and flanked by cast-iron stove figures of George Washington and Jenny Lind (mistakenly referred to as Martha Washington), leads into Azalea Woods. This wooden structure also came from Latimeria. The siting of the Washington figure was initially a whimsy and did not take on any compositional significance until the balancing female figure was acquired years later. This entire Iris Garden complex was visible from Ruth du Pont's bedroom windows.

Leading to the northeast from the conservatory is a path ending in a small, round garden that Marian called the Box Scroll Garden after its elaborate boxwood parterre that was seasonally enhanced with spring bulbs, summer bedding plants, and autumn chrysanthemums (this page). She cleverly used this circle as a fulcrum to turn the axis of the entire landscape design. Moving south from the Box Scroll Garden is the large terrace with poplar and beech trees that connects to the Italianate staircase and 1902 planting beds. To the north is the March Walk, on the way to the Pinetum and Azalea Woods. In her landscape design,

Two in-progress views of the installation of the Box Scroll Garden. c. 1930.

This 90-degree turn, pulling together the flagstone terraces and paths near the house and the naturalistic landscape of the March Bank, is one of the most successful aspects of Coffin's plan. The lower photograph shows mock-ups of trees and shrubs to ensure correct placement.

Opposite, inset: The Blue Room, formerly Ruth Wales du Pont's bedroom, had views of the Iris Garden in the 1930s and this medley of Spanish bluebells and lavender, pink, and rose azaleas later. The textile fixtures in the room were changed with the seasons, as the succession of bloom in the landscape progressed.

Above: The window in Cecil Bedroom, formerly H. F. du Pont's bedroom, affords a view of the East Terrace and grand Italianate staircase. Floral needlework abounds in the room, where woodwork is painted a grayish green.

Right: The dining room porch with its Doric columns and balustrade overlooking the East Terrace. c. 1932.

A wisteria vine is being trained to grow up the farthest pier and column. The large beech in the photograph is one of the trees that du Pont was intent on saving.

Coffin not only joined the house and garden but also linked Winterthur's past, present, and future gardens. In the years that followed, Harry wandered deep into the woods for his inspiration, but he began the journey on a straight and narrow path that Marian had made for him.

POINTS OF VIEW

A striking architectural feature of the main house is the grand porch, soaring three stories on the extreme southeastern end of the building. People speak about the picturesque quality of the chimneys rising above the high-pitched roof and dormer windows. In functional terms, the porch is one of the most important transitional zones between the building and the terrace that du Pont and Coffin designed. At ground level a loggia opens directly onto the terrace. A winding stone stair within the loggia proceeds up one story to the porch next to the Du Pont Dining Room. Guests walked onto the porch from the dining room to enjoy the view, and occasionally the du Ponts and their friends dined at long tables set under mosquito netting in this quintessential indoor/outdoor space (page 114).

Rising two stories above the dining room porch, Doric columns support an upper terrace with a balustrade outside du Pont's bedroom suite on the seventh floor. The entire seventh floor of the house afforded a series of views and vistas of the garden and estate: Harry's bedroom window overlooked the Italianate staircase; his bath and his dressing room, the terrace; and his office/sitting room, where he received the house and estate managers each morning, had views of the Farm Hill dairy barns, fields, and cow pastures along Clenny Run. He began each day surrounded by the crowns of his beloved trees, looking out onto the estate.

Ruth du Pont's bedroom suite was also on the seventh floor, at the north end of the building. Her bedroom looked over the entrance forecourt and the great poplars on the lawn and into the woods to the north, where Azalea Woods and other subsidiary paths were located (page 115). Far to the west the Iris Garden and Latimeria Summerhouse were visible. Her dressing room and bath looked out over the conservatory roof toward the March Bank, where successive waves of flowers bloomed throughout March, April, and early May. The rooms of the du Pont daughters, Pauline Louise and Ruth Ellen, were also on the seventh floor.

A GARDENER IN THE PARLOR

By the time he reached his early twenties, after his training at Bussey Institution, Harry's color preferences had been strongly influenced by garden writers such as Gertrude Jekyll and other theorists and practitioners of the English Arts and Crafts movement who, through their many publications, sought to turn taste away from the highly colored palette of Victorian England toward more muted, restrained colors taken from nature.

Harry filled his garden notebooks with notations on color. His eye captured minute differences in tone and value. He observed the colors of flowers as they changed under varying light conditions throughout the day and at different points in the blooming cycle. The color combinations that occur throughout the year in the northeastern woodlands and meadows became his favorites. Earth tones and shades of green are the background colors in the garden; he adopted them as the backdrop for his indoor color schemes as well (page 118). When he began large-scale gardening on the March Bank and in Azalea Woods, the trees, landforms, and massed shrubs provided structure for his naturalistic compositions. These landscape elements functioned like walls in a room. The landscape suggested various plant communities and color schemes in the same way that interior spaces and paneling inspired particular decorative treatments.

There is no question that the color sensibility Harry developed by working in the garden carried over into his early decorating efforts. In 1923, when visiting Electra Havemeyer Webb's collection of American decorative and folk arts at Shelburne, Vermont, he was struck by pink Staffordshire displayed on a pine dresser, perhaps because it reminded him of a bed of flowers. Soon afterward he visited decorator and collector Henry Davis Sleeper's house, Beauport, in Gloucester, Massachusetts, and was similarly impressed with the period interiors. Harry stated repeatedly that these two experiences were central to his becoming interested in the decorative arts. Years later the Webb family donated to Winterthur the very dresser and Staffordshire that du Pont had seen in 1923, as a memorial to that crucial experience in his collecting career. Sleeper functioned as an early adviser to du Pont; certainly Sleeper's vision of a sequence of sharply conceptualized spaces survives in some rooms at Winterthur today. It is equally apparent, however, that after du Pont broke with Sleeper in 1931, he moved away from some of the dramatic effects that Sleeper incorporated in his interiors. Perhaps du Pont tired of the more theatrical leitmotives: secret staircases, spectral lighting, loud color juxtapositions, and jejune historical commemoration. Only a few rooms at Winterthur remain associated with historical figures; at Beauport, each room has a tight historical identity, which Sleeper dilated upon in the course of his house tours.

Du Pont preferred a more indirect way of inviting movement through his spaces. While plotting paths through the woods and garden transition areas, Harry learned pacing and sequencing. He laid paths and arranged groupings of plantings with the expectation that visitors would discover the implied route, stopping at certain locations to examine specific

In the Walnut Room, the paneling has a grayish glazed surface over older, crumbly paint layers that overtly suggest the texture of the rough, mossy bark of the chamaecyparis.

Du Pont's displays of ceramics in the Blue Staffordshire Room parallel his massing of bulbs on the March Bank to a surprising degree. The garden photo of scilla, chionodoxa, and a few daffodils was taken in late March.

Near left: The Philadelphia Bedroom and the Patuxent Vestibule, with their Chinese wallpapers and pale blue woodwork, epitomize the interior garden rooms seen throughout the museum.

The Gold and White Room features an oriental birdcage at the window that whimsically echoes the chinoiserie Latimeria Summerhouse in the vista beyond.

The Port Royal Parlor is dressed for spring in yellow silk damask covers and curtains. In March, the East Terrace is already blooming with yellow witch-hazel and lavender Crocus tomasinianus.

blooms or plants or notice vistas. While it can be said that du Pont himself did not design any baroque axes in his garden in the manner of Marian Coffin, he used paths and vistas to help organize other parts of the garden, notably those through the Pinetum, various swaths cut through Azalea Woods toward the golf course, and, later, those in the Sycamore Area and on Oak Hill. This structure, however, is submerged in the drama of color combinations of flowers coming into bloom across the landscape throughout the year.

Despite color sequencing and the shifting emphasis of strategically placed plants coming into bloom, nowhere in the naturalistic garden areas that du Pont designed is there a single spectacular tree, shrub, or bank that stands out from the rest in an obvious manner. Herein resides the origin of what later became one of his decorating axioms: "It's one of my first principles that if you go into a room . . . and right away see something, then you must realize that it shouldn't be in the room." In creating rooms or gardens, he avoided focal points and masterworks, either man-made or horticultural, in favor of harmonious ensembles.

INDOOR/OUTDOOR

Du Pont's acute color perception is suggested by the forty-eight different shades of green used on paneling and walls throughout the house. Not only do the greens differ but their treatments vary. Some rooms have extremely complex glazing over paint to modify or soften the color. Browns range from painted earth colors to unpainted pine or mahogany paneling used in a limited number of rooms. The paucity of wood with transparent finishes (as opposed to painted wood) is notable, considering the 1930s American taste for English stripped-pine or limed-oak paneling.

Against these colors du Pont grouped ceramics and textiles to set up color contrasts or conscious bipolar or triadic color relationships. Du Pont was an avid collector of ceramics. He used them in his everyday dining arrangements, but he was primarily fascinated by colors. In the period rooms, he displayed ceramics in masses that recapitulated the color effects he used in banks of flowers in the garden. This decorating strategy is evident in the Spatterware Hall, Dresser Room, and Lebanon Room. A remarkable example of juxtaposing dark brown with other colors is the Blackwell Vestibule, where mahogany wainscoting, soft bluish green oriental wallpaper, and bottle-green silks are combined in a resonant manner repeated in the Philadelphia Bedroom (page 119).

Textiles also brought nature's colors indoors. During the Great Depression many country houses in England and France emptied their wardrobes of antique textiles, and they became available in quantity. A practice that was popular then but is frowned upon today

was the dismantling of antique dresses to reuse the silks for upholstery covers. Although some dress silks survived in the form of uncut bolts, most had been made into dresses, and the cloth displayed faded, soft colors that attracted du Pont's eye. He wanted muted, subtly modulated interiors that gave the impression of great age, and these faded fabrics were central to the desired effects.

Once he reached his stride as a decorator in the 1930s, du Pont could rapidly pull together the base color of a room, ceramics, glass, furniture, and textiles into compositions that had great potential for variation. So voracious was his collecting that he extended seasonal changes of textiles, both to display recent acquisitions and to express the seasons themselves. By changing curtains and slipcovers, he could have two or more rooms in one. Eventually du Pont slated between two and four textile changes for many rooms during the course of the year, which his assistant, George Colman, recorded in a "textile change book" formulated in 1946 and reformulated as they thought of new ideas. Although the du Ponts lived in Florida from February to late March and on Long Island during July and August, Harry stopped at Winterthur during his commutes to check on all the doings, aesthetic and otherwise.

Flower arrangements added another dimension to room decoration. The staff maintained several greenhouses and a large cutting garden to ensure a steady supply of flowers throughout the year. Large vases were usually filled with one kind of flower, with as many as twenty-five vases appearing in a single room during parties. For many members of the Winterthur staff, an enduring memory is that point during du Pont's morning ritual when he gave instructions about which place settings and linens were to be used for the lunch and dinner tables that day, chosen to coordinate with the flowers in bloom.

Yet another pervasive aspect to the decorating of the house was du Pont's use of artificial landscapes—generally European and oriental wallpapers, paintings, or needlework wall coverings that depicted landscapes. The Dining Room Cross Hall and Library Stairhall were once furnished with French landscape papers from the early nineteenth century. The Chinese Parlor, Blackwell Vestibule, Philadelphia Bedroom, and Patuxent Vestibule contain oriental landscape wallpapers or textiles. In this house where vistas of the surrounding landscape are omnipresent, du Pont still felt compelled to add landscapes in hallways, reinforcing the association of the interiors with nature.

In a few rooms, du Pont toyed with relationships between objects in the rooms and vistas through the windows. In the Gold and White Room, an oriental birdcage hanging in the window echoes the Latimeria Summerhouse in the distance (page 121). In the Imlay Room, a trumpet vine growing on the facade outside the room is echoed in flowering vines on wallpaper in the room. These humorous juxtapositions were grace notes to the main historical and stylistic themes developed through the selection and placement of objects.

Perhaps the ultimate interplay of interior and exterior resides in two evocative parallels we can intuit, but not prove, to have been du Pont's intention. One is the identification of similar color contrasts and triads in period rooms and the garden. The second is a subtle coordination of colors used to decorate rooms with flowers that bloomed outside the rooms at certain seasons. Flowers that thrive on the terrace along the east facade of the building are predominantly yellow in the late winter and yellow and lavender throughout the spring. Many of the major rooms on that side, notably the Port Royal Parlor and Chestertown Room, are furnished in yellow in the spring and autumn (page 121). The Blue Room overlooks clear pink azaleas and Spanish bluebells that bloom together in early May. During the early 1930s, when the modern-day Peony Garden was a large iris garden visible from the Blue Room, it appeared to be a sea of blue in April and May. Another wonderful example is the Patuxent Room, on the sixth floor, with its green walls and predominantly green textile fixtures, which is surrounded by the upper lawns with gigantic forest trees (page 124).

In Henry Francis du Pont's great house museum, distinctions between past and present and indoors and outdoors are intentionally blurred. Marian Coffin's elegant landscape architecture married a rather ungainly structure to its site, seamlessly reconciling house and garden. Du Pont's most successful rooms and garden areas are spectacular yet restrained, self-contained compositions that harmonize with their surroundings. They are a joy to be in, yet suggest deeper levels of meaning, especially the relationship between nature and art. At Winterthur, one is sometimes in the house museum but *always* in the garden.

Overleaf left: The resonant greens of the Patuxent Room reflect vistas of the museum lawn visible on three sides of the room, making this one of the most spectacular instances of the indoor/outdoor relationship at Winterthur.

Overleaf right: The orange, tan, and brown decor of the Maple Room is an obvious play on the autumn foliage palette.

Postscript
THE BEST-LAID PLANS

In 1928 Harry wrote to Marian Coffin:

> I don't propose to build this addition [to the house] until some time next spring, but . . . I am getting all the material on hand before doing a stroke of work in order to rush the house through in about six months.

Two years later he wrote again:

> They promised to have all the scaffolding down from the library wing of the house and also the east facade of the old and new house. In that way we will be able to lay out all those complicated steps, walks, etc.

In 1931 he explained to Marian:

> The house is practically finished, although it may not look so when you see it—but every curtain material and chair material is settled upon and ordered and the work is being done, and every color of paint has been selected, and every piece of furniture put in place.

In 1939 he informed a friend:

> We . . . move to New York the 2nd of January, as I am going to put some more rooms on the fourth floor and it is going to make a lot of dust.

And again:

> I am making lots of changes in the house, which will be finished, I hope, sometime or other.

In 1948 he wrote once more:

> I will certainly be thankful to have the thing done as I was always afraid I would pass out before it was completed.

Many visitors to Winterthur remark upon this view through the Port Royal Entrance Hall to the East Terrace. The eyes of gardeners, especially, sail past the beautiful wallpaper and Chippendale furniture to the great outdoors.

HARRY'S OTHER GARDEN

Paul Hensley

> Mama and I visited the cows after dinner. You will find their stable
> greatly improved by two new stanchions.
> HENRY ALGERNON TO H. F. DU PONT 1893

> Somehow or other, as I think I said before, I've always been interested in this
> sort of thing [breeding cattle], and I think I'll keep on with it.
> H. F. DU PONT 1962

On an August evening in 1930, some ten months after Black Tuesday plunged Wall Street and much of the nation into financial chaos, Winterthur Farms suffered a smaller-scale disaster. About 5:30 P.M. on that fateful summer day, a workman milking cows in the eastern portion of the dairy barn noticed smoke wafting from the hayloft above. He sounded the alarm, but by the time workmen rescued all 100 cows from the barn, flames had totally engulfed the building. The ominous glow soon could be seen for miles around. Despite the efforts of Winterthur's farmers and men from six surrounding rural fire companies, by the following dawn only three silos remained of the 333-foot structure (page 131). Unofficial estimates put the loss at $250,000.

This vignette of local history might go unnoticed except for its implications, which threatened to jeopardize the very existence of the Winterthur herd and the continuity of the farm. Henry Francis du Pont had considered reducing the size of the herd in response to financial uncertainties caused by the stock market crash, a possibility that seemed all the more prudent since the 1928 enlargement of his house and garden was still unfinished.

Because of the destruction on Farm Hill, du Pont found himself at a crucial crossroads that demanded a decision: regroup and rebuild or abandon the herd altogether. Within a week, M. S. Prescott, editor of *Holstein-Friesian World*, sent him an encouraging letter con-

One of the remaining barns is framed by 'Firefly,' H. F. du Pont's "lacquer red azalea" on Oak Hill. Such views afford a glimpse into Winterthur's past, when house, farm, and garden were closely intertwined.

cerning the loss of the Winterthur dairy barn: "While . . . materials of constructions can always be replaced," he counseled, "the work you have accomplished along constructive breeding lines would have meant a staggering loss to the whole industry if it had been wiped out." In November 1931, having been misinformed that du Pont was planning to get rid of the herd, Frank Price, business manager of the magazine, complimented him again on his fine work in developing the Winterthur herd and asserted, "It almost seems like a calamity for us to hear you say that you are dropping out."

Du Pont had no intention of quitting. He immediately responded: "I am so keenly interested in the development and advancement of the Holstein breed . . . that I could not bear to have a closing out sale." Instead, "[I] have been very carefully considering how I could run my establishment along much more simple lines. I must confess that the present economic conditions have made such a step more imperative."

With a strategy of simplicity in mind, du Pont reacted to the Farm Hill conflagration not by abandoning the herd but rather by restructuring dairy operations and redoubling efforts to attain even better production. Three motivations informed this response: his desire to achieve perfection in whatever endeavor he undertook, his realization that success required comprehensive planning within existing realities, and his willingness to experiment in order to achieve excellence. In the words of Howard S. Lattomus, a longtime employee at Winterthur Farms who became superintendent in the mid-1960s, du Pont made no plans lightly: "He had to have the best."

Indeed, this had been the case all along. When Henry Algernon allowed his son to take over management of Winterthur Farms in 1914, the younger du Pont announced his intention to sell off the existing, largely nonpurebred, mixed herd of Guernsey and Holstein cattle and to focus on developing a nearly perfect breed of Holsteins. In approving the plan, Henry Algernon predicted, "Your idea is a splendid one which will be of benefit to humanity." Harry immediately began studying works of English cattle breeders as well as published reports regarding successful generational interbreeding of sibling rats. He realized that perfecting a better breed of Holsteins required a thorough knowledge of animal nutrition, employment of special testing to determine butterfat content of Holstein milk, and testing of cows before registry to determine production volume. Advanced registry testing began at Winterthur in 1914, and testing on an annual basis began in 1920. Under this regimen, du Pont had a control group of Holsteins fed and milked four times a day by an elite corps of milkers who were paid "according to [their] ability to wring every drop of milk from [their] charge[s]." The volume of milk was recorded on weigh sheets.

In June 1915 the board of directors of the Holstein-Friesian Association of America responded favorably to Harry's application for membership, as they had to Henry Algernon's in 1895, and unanimously elected him a life member. Soon afterward he began purchasing the best specimens of female and sire Holsteins from various sources including Moyer Farm in upstate New York, Schroeder Farms in Minnesota, and Allamuchy and Tranquility farms in New Jersey. By 1926 the Winterthur herd consisted of more than 300 registered Holsteins, and average annual milk production exceeded 11,000 pounds per cow. That same year du Pont received national recognition from the Holstein-Friesian Association for his achievements in breeding.

The herd provided a cohesive link between the agricultural and dairying components of the farm and also quickly secured du Pont's reputation within the national Holstein community. In January 1918, *Black and White Record*, a national weekly journal devoted to Holstein news, made plans for a feature article on Delaware champion herds. Two of du Pont's cows had recently been acclaimed as the highest butter producers in the state, and the editors wanted to publish photographs to "give these great cows all the credit that is

Dairy barn complex. c. 1928.

Garden watchers will spot young conifers in the Pinetum, begun in 1918, in the upper right-hand corner of the photograph.

due them for their performance." Du Pont availed himself of the *Black and White* network, as well as other channels, to advertise and sell young bulls and cows from his herd. Having seen one of the advertisements, J. T. Axtell, a veterinarian from Newton, Kansas, inquired about the price of "a *good* bull this fall." Du Pont's reply demonstrated his pride in the herd: Sir Inka Prilly Segis, son of the herd sire, was a perfect candidate. "We have every

Virginia creeper traces an autumn pattern on these Farm Hill silos.

confidence in his making good. . . . His photograph shown on his pedigree has not been touched up in any way. . . . He is a show bull in every respect. His hide is of the finest tissue."

Henry Algernon had purchased a few registered Holsteins in the early 1900s, but Harry pursued development of a purebred herd seriously and, in a sense, saw its creation in much the same way as he would later perceive antiques collecting.

H. F. du Pont recognized that an aggressive breeding and dairying program required adequate facilities and as early as 1915 corresponded with Elmer J. Humphries, partner in the upstate New York firm of Stafford and Humphries, specialists in concrete construction and experienced in building dairy barns. For Winterthur, Humphries proposed a barn with reinforced concrete floors for the safety of cattle in case of fire, fireproof doors at hay shoots, and an elaborate ventilating and temperature-control system—in short, state-of-the-art barn construction. Du Pont brought Humphries down from McGraw, New York, to manage the construction of a group of buildings on Farm Hill, including a large dairy barn and creamery, a test barn, a calf barn, heifer and bull barns, six barns for wintering young stock, an ice plant, and a facility for bacteriological tests on milk (opposite). After construction of the complex was finished in 1917, du Pont hired Humphries to serve as superintendent of Winterthur Farms and subsequently added further staff, including a farm manager, resident veterinarian, dairy manager, and herdsman.

When du Pont created the herdsman position in February 1919 by hiring J. R. Danks away from Osceola Farm in Cranford, New Jersey, he reemphasized: "I am an enthusiastic breeder of Holsteins and am putting a great deal of money and time into this proposition, and it is needless to say that I will look to you in every case to take care of my interests and will expect you to put forth your all to make the results obtained worth while."

By the time H. F. du Pont became owner of Winterthur in 1927, the estate was more than 2,200 acres of rolling farmland ranging from Kennett Pike to the south, Center Meeting and Guyencourt roads to the east, Brandywine Creek and Rockland Road to the north, and Kirk and Montchanin roads to the west. Comprised of several agricultural tracts including Negendank, Armor, Chandler, Rockland, and Montchanin farms, Winterthur Farms included some 90 houses for families working on the farm and embraced a nearly self-sufficient community with its own water supply, crops, shops, post office, and railroad freight station.

Under du Pont's able administration, Winterthur Farms supplied meat, fruit, vegetables, and dairy products to the Winterthur community and to his own tables at Winterthur; Boca Grande, Florida; and Southampton, Long Island. Winterthur Farms was Harry's "other garden"; it stood in practical relief to his lovely naturalistic garden and served the basic needs of Winterthur and the wider community. Just as he sensed an important design and aesthetic connection between his antiques-filled period rooms and the garden vistas beckoning beyond, du Pont also realized that a dynamic organic synthesis existed between farm and garden, each merging subtly and sometimes imperceptibly into the other (page 128). Writing to a fellow member of the American Primrose Society in 1963, he described his new Quarry Garden and "a little stream fenced off from my Holsteins for my Japonicas." Most important of all, the peripheral farmlands provided an unobtrusive but effective barrier protecting the security and integrity of both farm and garden from possible subsequent changes in the neighboring landscape.

In a very real sense, then, the disastrous barn fire of 1930 had potentially severe consequences for broader reasons than just the dairy and breeding operations. Had du Pont decided to sell off the herd, much of the farm's reason for being would have evaporated, and a vital part of Winterthur might have been abandoned early on. By his own admission, the fire made him realize that he "would have to do something rather drastic before long." As it turned out, he tried a new experiment that saved the herd and resulted in production rates that rocked the Holstein-Friesian community.

Late in 1931 du Pont began a gradual program of shifting the Winterthur herd from a Class A regimen of four feedings and milkings per day to a Class C, or advanced registry, regimen of twice-daily feedings and milkings. This saved money in terms of lower feed and labor costs, and reduction of the herd also lessened testing expenses. Moreover, the program reflected du Pont's realization that "big league" testing involving forced feeding four times a day neither mirrored the small-farm origins of the herd nor matched the potential market that Winterthur breeding stock was trying to reach. The new regimen more accurately revealed the production capability of the herd and the importance of bloodline in affecting production levels. In spite of reservations within the dairy community that the new program might lower production levels and perhaps even compromise the reputation of the Winterthur herd, in May 1933 one of the herd achieved a new world record for butterfat production that exceeded even the Class A 1,000-pound standard.

Heartened by this accomplishment, which created a sensation among Holstein-Friesian circles, du Pont began planning for a new dairy barn in 1934. In October his financial adviser, J. Frank Otwell, asserted that the new barn would be a good investment "whether you sell . . . milk [to the outside] or merely have it for the big house and the [New York] apartment." In addition, Otwell estimated that a new barn would save the labor of at least two men: "There is a lot of time lost in having to bring the cows from the various barns up to the bulls, as well as in getting ensilage to the cows." Moreover, he warned, "You cannot sell baby's milk [much longer] without a new barn, due to the inspectors and the conditions." With the proposed structure, Otwell concluded, du Pont would be able to sell "milk for cash to the big house, the apartment, the [Winterthur] boarding house, all the people on the place, and the special baby's milk to Wilmington, to say nothing of having a decent place in which to show the stock." By 1935 work was finished, and in March of that year Winterthur Farms began mixing its own feeds in lieu of purchasing ready-mixed ones.

In April 1935 the Holstein-Friesian Association's superintendent of advanced registry notified du Pont that the Winterthur herd had received recognition on the 1934 honor list. "Not only does the herd lead in total number of places shown on the list for the year," the superintendent reported, "but it also stands high in the number of first places, and I want to compliment you on this extremely fine showing." In 1936 the Winterthur herd again led the honor list with six first-place winners; four years later it took forty-seven places, including nine firsts. The superintendent praised du Pont on "a remarkable showing of which you may be very proud in competition with other breeders testing for Advanced Registry throughout the United States." In the 1940s and 1950s the Winterthur herd continued to win distinction, including the first-place prize awarded to Winterthur Zeus Fobes Cajalo in 1951 for a superior score earned during the year for a single lactation.

The Winterthur Farms herd also achieved a reputation of national proportions in science; in the early 1950s the University of Nebraska began an experimental artificial-insemination program, which included a careful study of Winterthur's breeding methods. Three years later the university published a comprehensive study of the breeding program, including analyses of herd production levels, for distribution to key agricultural centers around the world. The authors of the publication gave du Pont high praise for initiative and persistence. In 1963 and 1964 the Holstein-Friesian Association of America bestowed on du Pont its Progressive Breeders Registry Award, an honor for which only "a very small percentage of the breeders of Holstein-Friesian cattle have qualified . . . over the years."

By the early 1960s—when Winterthur Farms included 1,070 acres, a milking herd of 74 cows complemented by 93 heifers, 3 herd sires, and 5 young bulls—du Pont and farm superintendent Leslie Potts, who took over operations when E. J. Humphries died in 1952, had spent nearly a decade assessing the future, having been prompted by frequent year-end losses and changing tax structures. As early as January 1953 Potts reported to a Maryland butter industry consultant that "we are making butter at a considerable loss," and he expressed appreciation for any suggestions about how Winterthur could increase its yield. In March of that year du Pont responded to Potts's farm budget proposal by asking whether it might be possible to realize substantial savings if "we only had steers and nothing but pasture lands and alfalfa" and whether the farm might be able to sell the hay at reasonable profits.

Probably adding weight to the serious considerations regarding farm reductions was du Pont's 1956 implementation of a pension plan for Winterthur Farms employees and his personal staff. Moreover, in February 1963 du Pont advised Potts that "there is a strong likelihood that the new tax law may triple my taxes. From now on we must make every effort to cut down on all my expenses." Among other questions, he asked Potts for statistics on the total cost per year of feed for the various farm animals. Later that month Potts wrote to du Pont that he had given a great deal of thought to cutting costs. "I have been studying our debts and credits pretty thoroughly," he reported, "and have not drawn any conclusions at this time except for the Dairy. If we were to eliminate the Main Dairy we would retain for the Test Barn about 18 milking cows . . . about 10 bred heifers . . . and probably two herd sires."

Potts had had his own vision of what Winterthur Farms might become, and early in 1956 he sent du Pont the outlines of an intriguing plan that advocated using the farm as a practical teaching laboratory under the aegis of a study program in cooperation with the University of Delaware. "Winterthur is synonymous with antique furniture, beautiful landscaped gardens, fine purebred Holstein cattle and fertile farm land. Through the Winterthur Corporation you have made it possible for the continued existence of the antique furniture and the gardens. It would seem plausible to include in the Corporation planning a service to the agricultural minded public." Through collaboration with the university, Potts continued, "It is conceivable that with the assets of Winterthur's land, cattle, and buildings (features lacking at the university), a permanent program could be worked out valuable to the development of the expanded agricultural course now under consideration at the University."

Characteristically, du Pont responded by asking a host of questions regarding the potential impact on the estate if the program were actually put into operation. Potts prepared a more detailed plan that he shared with du Pont and one of the deans at the University of Delaware. Subsequently du Pont asked Potts to estimate the cost and "what, if any, financial help or labor will come from the University?" Having sent an amended report to du Pont, Potts received a letter of March 26 from Boca Grande in which du Pont thanked him for the concise outline but delayed further discussion of the proposal with words that demonstrate the close and sometimes competitive connection of the farm and garden: "I do

A sweeping planting of the Narcissus poeticus 'Queen of the Nile' along Clenny Run directs a view of cloudlike daffodil beds, a small waterfall, and a farmhouse. This is the serene entrance to Winterthur. The main drive over the bridge is not visible from this vantage point. The roadway was lowered into the landscape so as not to interrupt the rolling piedmont terrain.

136

not think I will be able to talk to you about this plan for a full month after I get back as my time will be taken up by meetings and details of the spring's plantings."

Potts continued to raise the issue and in October 1959 drew up a future development plan that contained provisions for educational scholarships in conjunction with the University of Delaware and general public and school tours. He advocated that Winterthur Corporation hold title to the farm properties and that several functions, including farming, dairying, forestry, property management and maintenance, and student farming visitations, fall under the jurisdiction of a property committee reporting to the Winterthur museum director. Although schoolchildren regularly visited the farm, Potts's full plan never reached fruition, perhaps in large measure because du Pont believed that management of such a program would constitute a heavy burden on the corporation.

In November 1959 du Pont had his last will and testament revised. Included in that codicil was a provision for Winterthur Corporation to receive his "herd of Holstein cattle and all other livestock, poultry, horses, carriages, carts, harness and stable equipment, and all dairy, farm, agricultural and other implements" at the time of his death. Looking to the future, and cer-

H. F. du Pont visiting his bulls in 1957. Photographed by Cornell Capa for Life *magazine.*

tainly with the good of the museum and the herd in mind, he made sure that the following was included: "In the interest of preserving and realizing the maximum value of such herd of Holstein cattle, I recommend that Winterthur Corporation arrange for the sale of such herd promptly after my death or promptly after receiving the possession thereof from my Executors in the distribution of my estate."

For the rest of his life, however, Henry Francis du Pont continued to achieve excellence in his herd program. In November 1968 the executive secretary of the Holstein-Friesian Association of America notified him that once again he had earned the Progressive Breeders Registry Award: "This is the most coveted recognition of breeder achievement accorded by our Association. It is all the more significant, therefore, that you have qualified for this award for the seventh year. Please accept my heartiest congratulations and best wishes for your continued success in achieving the goals established for this award."

Postscript

THE LIFE OF A DAIRY FARMER

In June of 1948 Harry described his spring and summer activities to a longtime friend:

Dear Johnny:

I am very glad to get your letter and much interested in your news. I was making out a list of my summer visitors a few days ago and I was hoping you would surely come.

We were in Florida for two months where we had perfect weather and got back here just before Easter. I always like to be home for the Easter services in our church. For two months we have had countless people staying with us—some to see the house and some to see our azaleas. I have specialized in our azaleas for many years now. . . . Some varieties start blooming early in April and the late ones are good till almost the end of May. About a thousand people from the Pennsylvania Horticultural Society motored from around Philadelphia to see them one day. Then five hundred people came in special cars from the New York Botanical Gardens, and there have been countless small garden clubs, horticulturists, other azalea growers, etc.

Ruth went to Hot Springs, Virginia, for a two weeks' rest and I spent a few days there with her. There are wonderful hot springs there which are very relaxing and good for one.

We go to Southampton July 1st for eight to ten weeks. Alfred, Pauline and the grandchildren spend August with us there. Ruth Ellen and George are well and they are to be abroad for two months this summer.

You may be interested to know that I once more top the Holstein-Friesian Honor list for the year 1947. This time I have seventy one points more than 1946, and better than anyone has ever done. I am afraid this time I have reached the peak; however, one never knows. . . .

I have made a Visitors Entrance to the Museum coming into the court [with four different house facades] by various halls from the outside.

I did appreciate your writing and here's wishing you and Barbara all best wishes. Drop me a line when you get settled.

Sincerely yours,
Harry

GARDEN FOR A "COUNTRY PLACE MUSEUM"

Denise Magnani

Here I have been these forty years learning the language
of these fields that I may the better express myself.

HENRY DAVID THOREAU 1857

My work is in the garden.

H. F. DU PONT 1967

On October 30, 1951, the Henry Francis du Pont Winterthur Museum was opened to the public. After the crowning triumph of seeing his life's work memorialized for posterity, the seventy-one-year-old founder could have been content to rest on his laurels. That wasn't his plan. He puckishly told a reporter from the *New York Times* dispatched to cover the event, "I'm only a visitor at the museum these days, but I'm still Head Gardener at Winterthur."

Several months before the opening, the du Ponts had moved to a new house located at the base of the museum lawn along Clenny Run where the Bidermann farmhouse, later a guest cottage, had been. From there, it was just a short walk to "visit" the museum, which Harry did several times a day when he was at Winterthur. The farm, the garden, and their respective staffs remained under his direction.

For many years the du Ponts had generously shared Winterthur's treasures with countless scholars, students, collectors, horticulturists, friends, and acquaintances. The Board of Trustees modeled the initial museum tour structure after Harry and Ruth's gracious entertaining regimen: four visitors accompanied by a guide toured a selection of period rooms in the morning and then had lunch in the Charleston Dining Room. They could see the remaining rooms in the afternoon. So that the public might also enjoy the garden at its height of bloom, a museum-garden combination ticket was made available beginning in 1952; soon, Winterthur in Spring became a Wilmington tradition.

*Most artists develop a knack for seizing opportunities and making the most of them, artistically speaking. Just a little south of Winterthur (which is in zone 6) native redbuds (*Cercis canadensis*) create a mauve haze in April, when their unusual sessile blossoms appear along the branches of the small trees. Harry borrowed the idea of a purple mist to entice visitors to walk through the Sycamore Area. In the center of the photo, the rounder, darker, small redbud is the species from China,* Cercis chinensis.

Hundreds of letters in the Winterthur archives attest to the fact that H. F. du Pont, with tireless enthusiasm, personally accompanied innumerable guests on tours through his garden. The experience seems to have moved, even overwhelmed, many of these walking companions. Of course, Harry was the ideal garden guide. He always knew which flowers were blooming and could answer any questions his guests might have.

When the public began to walk in the garden on their own, however, Harry quickly realized that most people were unaccustomed to a garden like his. The beds of brightly colored annuals so typical of early twentieth-century American display gardens were nowhere to be found. Instead, his paths wound among naturalistic plant groupings and evanescent color schemes. Harry decided that visitors would benefit from a little unobtrusive guidance, and so he ordered a general garden introduction and map prepared. He asked his carpenters to fashion simple wooden arrows on stakes that could be placed to lead visitors to areas in bloom—green going into the garden, white going back to the parking lot. He personally supervised the changing of the arrows every few days in spring to keep pace with the performance of his choreography of bloom.

In February 1955 Harry wrote to his dear friend Marian Coffin, offering her a job: "I would like you, if you are not too busy with your spring work, to make a preliminary sketch of an April Shrub Garden. There the public must have masses, to see things."

Harry knew that everyone loved Azalea Woods, and he assumed it was the exuberant abundance of blooms in May that thrilled visitors. He decided to create a similar effect in April. His chosen site was the level area near the Pinetum where the tennis court and croquet lawn were languishing, unused.

Without waiting for Marian's reply he provided her with the beginnings of a plant list. He thought that a natural transition to the proposed area would be an extension of the Quince Walk, which he had installed through the Pinetum in the late 1930s. That gave him the idea of using "two absolutely gigantic" *Chaenomeles* 'Appleblossom' (a flowering quince cultivar that was a du Pont family favorite) and "of course some smaller ones" that were already growing on the property and could be transplanted. He also suggested the flowering cherry 'Hally Jolivette,' and the rare *Spiraea* x *arguta*, the most free flowering of the early spireas, because it bloomed with the quince.

On du Pont's April blooming list that year he checked off candidates for relocation to a shrub garden that was to be "all pink and white," as he put it. Given his presumption of moving plants that already had a twelve- to fifteen-foot spread, one comment in his letter to Coffin is puzzling at first: "This is a permanent planting, not for immediate effect." It certainly seemed that the April Shrub Garden would rise from the level playing field more quickly than other areas at Winterthur that evolved over many years. But there was more to it. Harry was alerting Marian to a change in his thinking. It was no longer sufficient for the fruits of their collaboration to please only themselves. The project was for the public, and at ages seventy-five and seventy-nine, respectively, Winterthur's head gardener and the "best landscape architect" might not get the chance to do it over. This design had to be "for all time."

Although Marian had developed a chronic cardiac condition and had reduced her practice, she responded, "It gave me a real thrill to receive your letter about doing the new planting at Winterthur." In April she traveled to Delaware with her assistant, Clara Coffey, and walked the Winterthur garden with Harry as she had done so many times before.

Coffin once wanted to write a book called "The Seeing Eye," by which she meant the ability to visualize an area as it would be in the future, after a planting had been installed. She possessed this useful ability, as did Harry. After they "talked through" an area, she was the one who put their visualizations on paper in the form of a planting plan.

In May she submitted two designs for consideration. Du Pont preferred the simpler scheme, essentially two concentric circles of shrubs, broken by north-south and east-west axes and with a strong feeling of enclosure. Letters debating the merits of various plants flew back and forth between their offices all summer. Some were very playful, as when du Pont addressed Coffin as "Anty Kerria" because she objected to the yellow *Kerria japonica* he had proposed. Harry and Marian had fun in their work; perhaps this, along with mutual respect and a shared vital interest, was the key to their compatibility throughout their long careers.

Harry suggested many changes to Marian's plan. In their collaborations, final plant selection had always been his prerogative. During the work on this project, Marian's uncertain health prevented her from visiting the site again until much later in the design process, and Harry had to take up the slack. Although the two friends were forced to conduct a long-distance dialogue, they understood each other's habits of thought so well that the April Shrub Garden expresses both of their personalities, yet is perfectly unified.

As usual, Coffin contributed the "bones" of the piece. Clarity resulted from the axial structure of the design and definition from the low evergreen hedge, *Lonicera pileata*. Towering evergreens in the neighboring Pinetum provided a dramatic backdrop. Her design took the form of a garden room, a twentieth-century innovation exemplified by American expatriate Sir Lawrence Johnston's Hidcote, and Sissinghurst, created by Vita Sackville-West and Sir Harold Nicolson.

Sometimes in a garden room seeing through the walls is the point. A window to the Sycamore Area is made of lavender princess tree blooms and the vivid pink azalea 'Homebush.' Across Garden Lane are pastel Meyer lilacs and, slightly left of center in the photograph, the fragrant fringe of the small tree Chionanthus virginicus, or old man's beard.

Inset: The Sundial Garden is a room made of flowers. Against the pyramidal dawn redwood and other conifers in the Pinetum, lavender lilac hybrids are shown to great advantage. White (or near-white) flowers are yet to come into full bloom in the tight sequencing that characterizes this planting: lilac 'Primrose,' the sweetly fragrant bladdernut (Staphlea colchica), and azaleas 'Amethystina' and R. mucronatum.

In February 1955, the same month he commissioned the April Shrub Garden, Harry visited England and saw the Nicolsons' garden. At Sissinghurst, the idea of a garden room was meant almost literally. In their famous collaboration, Harold planned architectural spaces enclosed by clipped hedges or brick walls that opened onto one another just as rooms in a house do, and Vita furnished the rooms with an exquisite, sophisticated, and romantic tangle of perennials, shrubs, vines, and trees. Their garden style was an elaboration of Gertrude Jekyll's genius in glorifying the cottage garden. In the Coffin–du Pont version at Winterthur, Marian decided where the walls of the room should be, and Harry chose what they should be made of: magnolias, quince, cherries, crabapples, viburnums, spireas, azaleas, lilacs, and roses (page 145).

The timing of Harry's visit to England and the inception of his new garden may have been a mere coincidence, but in early May, the northeast quadrant of the April Shrub Garden seems to be a sly homage to Sissinghurst's famous White Garden. Harry planted a "white walk" of pure white azaleas; the palest yellow lilac 'Primrose'; the azalea 'Amethystina,' whose flower is white suffused with a faint blush of lavender; the pearlbush called 'The Bride'; and several other shrubs with white flowers. In Vita's garden, white flowers play off perennials with silvery or gray foliage. At Winterthur Harry just happened to have some light green and gray foliage to work against—a huge, undulating Pfitzer juniper, an impossibly fast-growing dawn redwood, and a blue atlas cedar with a fifty-foot spread—all flourishing in his father's Pinetum.

TEMPUS FUGIT

The most fascinating aspect of the area under discussion is one that neither Harry nor Marian mentioned in their letters. The April Shrub Garden, for all its aura of soft informality, is tightly organized. It is obvious from the plan, or from a bird's-eye view, that however flowing and indeterminate the garden feels to someone within the space, the shrubs are arranged simply, in concentric circles. Although most of the plants are in bloom together in late April, they *come* into bloom in strict sequence, beginning at one end of the garden with the star magnolias—a different genus bursting forth every few days—and finishing at the other end with the late lilacs flowering beneath lavender princess trees (*Paulownia tomentosa*) in early May (pages 144–45).

Such precision could not be coincidental, but no great concern with sequencing is evident in Coffin's original plan. When she visited the proposed site for the garden, she decided that some existing star magnolias would be a logical point of departure. Naturally,

How can we resist the invitation to walk proffered by the fragrant lavender 'Winterthur' blossoms, especially when the thrilling azalea 'Firefly' is ahead? Oak Hill is a metaphor for the journey of life, of anticipation and adventure, of setting out optimistically and returning, satisfied. We cannot enjoy the garden unless we enter it, spend time, and go the distance. The garden reminds us that getting there is half the fun.

In the areas surrounding the Sundial Garden, H. F. du Pont proved that, for him, "color is the thing that really counts more than any other." The fuschia azalea is 'Hino-de-giri,' a red accompanied by the ever-present lavender, a lilac hybrid. This time they are joined by cerise redbuds. The foliage of the shrubs above the azaleas is still fresh enough to be called chartreuse, du Pont's favorite green for blending striking shades. In spring, the azaleas are red; the burning bush (Euonymus alata) above them is green. In autumn, the colors are reversed.

Inset: At the completion of a work, the beginning should be felt. Harry first broke out of the border by naturalizing the minor bulbs in the larger landscape. One of his last, best ideas was to link the gardens of a lifetime into one. The blue waves of scilla and chionodoxa carry the eye from the yellow and lavender of the Winterhazel Walk on the left to the white star magnolias and 'Wada's Memory' on the right. Traces remain in the Winterthur garden of every step Harry took in his evolution as a landscape designer.

she wanted to use plants that bloom throughout the month, and some of the changes and rearranging that Harry decided on later were probably his attempt to strengthen an orderly progression that was latently inherent in her design (pages 148–49).

The careful sequencing was an artistic representation of a natural phenomenon that had intrigued Harry since his childhood. Scott Weidensaul describes this phenomenon in his *Seasonal Guide to the Natural Year* (1992):

> In nature, timing is everything—the timing of the seasons, of courtship, of migration, of birth. Even though wild animals and plants cannot read the calendar, they respond to the changing length of daylight through the year. Coupled with other, subtle clues we do not fully understand, this signal allows nature to progress at a pace, and with a precision, that surprises many people when they first discover it.

Harry delighted in anticipating and noting these events each year. In his garden—and what is a garden if not a little world that we create to our liking?—he incorporated his own predictable seasonal markers.

During the last fifteen years of his work, what Harry called succession of bloom became, along with naturalism, movement, and color harmony, one of the fundamental organizing principles of his art. The reason the idea loomed so large in his mind may be as simple as his perception that the public always clamored to see something in bloom. As Shakespeare wrote in sonnet 15: "When I consider everything that grows/Holds in perfection but a little moment."

A naturalistic garden needs many little moments of perfection. The desire to ensure them may have inspired Harry's renewed emphasis on sequencing. For William Robinson and Gertrude Jekyll, especially, the necessity to have something always in bloom in the garden was an important philosophical principle underlying their theories. For Harry, creating a strict succession was an intellectual challenge, a puzzle, and a game. He began refining other areas started many years before, to extend the blooming time as long as possible without disrupting the main display or color scheme of each. He added lilies to Azalea Woods, wildflowers to the March Bank, and azaleas and rhododendrons throughout the garden. In 1962 he even nestled a "Once-a-Week Path" along the entire span of the Pinetum, creating it with new pink azalea cultivars he had been evaluating and arranging them to come into bloom one week apart from late April to mid June. Undoubtedly, the Winterthur garden is one of the most highly articulated embodiments of succession of bloom ever created.

If du Pont's new focus on succession was indeed motivated by a wish to please the public, it appears he was successful. Even though most visitors were probably unaware of the staggering complexity of succession of bloom on such a grand scale, they seemed to appreciate the green arrows, and they simply loved the garden.

A few years after the April Shrub Garden was completed, an armillary sundial that had graced Pauline du Pont's rose garden was moved there, and the garden that you could almost set your watch by became the Sundial Garden.

On February 14, 1956, Marian wrote to Harry:

> I would like very much to come down to Winterthur for one or two days and a night. I want to see in a "Friendly" way only, how the new garden looks and if I could make you any other ground cover suggestions—no charge! I feel better and quite a lot stronger than I did last year and would like to see a little of my work.

The visit on May 6 and 7 drained her:

> I . . . came back very sick and have been in bed ever since. The doctor was right, I should never have gone, but I enjoyed myself immensely, and hope I was a comfort to you. The doctor says my heart will be all right again after a couple of weeks' rest.

It was to be her last visit. She suffered a stroke on January 30 of the following year and died on February 2, 1957.

A HOST OF GOLDEN DAFFODILS = 18,000

Although H. F. du Pont significantly expanded the Winterthur garden after Marian Coffin died, he never again hired a landscape architect to help him. He continued to seek horticultural advice from experts and to give it when asked, since his reputation as a plantsman was growing. He relied more than ever on his garden staff, in what for many was a memorable and meaningful collaboration. He was a good manager. He discussed his plans with his staff; he sought their advice and took it; he held them to high standards, but if a mistake was made, it could always be fixed. Each gardener felt responsible for the garden's success.

In those years most of the garden staff addressed him as "Mr. du Pont" or "Mr. Harry" and very affectionately called him "the old man" when he wasn't around. They had to be careful—he was around a lot. Even on a day when nothing extraordinary was scheduled, he took two long walks in the garden, stopping to observe progress or to chat with the gardeners In the 1960s the workweek in the garden was Monday through Friday, and a half-day every other Saturday. David S. Richard, who came to work on the garden staff as a youngster and rose through the ranks to become a supervisor before his retirement in 1991, believes that

Overleaf left: Harry was aware of many theories about color, "a vast field in itself." He was "very fond of color" (not to overstate the case) and preferred to create ineffable garden pictures, leaving words to others. One such composition is the ruby horsechestnut (Aesculus splendens) with Preston hybrid lilacs and creamy white Chionanthus virginicus.

Overleaf right: Many poets, painters, and gardeners have romanticized forests and wildflower meadows. But the stage in forest succession known as an old-field meadow seems to be an acquired taste. Not to Harry. This dynamic image shows how he maximized the riches of a common roadside scene.

du Pont simply liked to have the crew around as much as possible and also felt an urgency to finish, to perfect the garden before he died.

It is to these gardeners that we owe what knowledge we have of du Pont's design process. He did not work from plans and never really articulated a design philosophy. He never claimed to be a garden designer, let alone an artist. It was Marian Coffin who insisted he was a "true artist."

Without Marian to provide the structure for a new planting, Harry looked to nature for it, or, rather, he used his considerable powers of imagination and visualization to see how the natural features of an area could be transformed into a satisfying space with the proper deletions and additions of plants. This was similar to the way the architectural features of a room suggested to him the most harmonious and suitable arrangement of furniture. Sometimes it worked the other way. A desirable plant often sent him in search of a site, or an object in pursuit of a setting.

At the same time that the April, or Sundial, Garden was being planned, the gardeners planted 18,000 daffodil bulbs in the golf course fairway just to the east. The huge cloudlike beds in distinctive interlocking shapes have become a hallmark of the Winterthur garden for many visitors. Daffodils are a perfect symbol of Winterthur's transition from private to public garden. Narcissus had always been one of Harry's favorite flowers, ever since he naturalized them in a grove of trees in 1902. Then, he collected bent twigs and sticks to guide the shapes of the beds. When the bulbs went into the golf course in 1955, it was in similar but greatly enlarged, more confident sweeps and arranged with branches that could be seen from a great distance.

The golf course daffodils come into bloom in late April and are visible from the Sundial Garden, which is also in full bloom by that time. Harry began to establish transitional plantings to link the areas he had created over the previous forty years. He encouraged the electric blue river of scilla and chionodoxa on the March Bank to flow into Azalea Woods. He removed shrubs and limbed up trees so that the spectacular Easter-blooming *Magnolia* 'Wada's Memory' in the Sundial Garden could beckon a visitor surrounded by the lavender and pale yellow haze of the Winterhazel Walk. He sited the April-blooming pink *Rhododendron fargesii* at one end of Azalea Woods to commune with the saucer magnolias his father had planted before he was born. Harry dissolved the boundaries between the garden areas, using sweeps of color to unify disparate elements, making them one.

In 1959 du Pont hired British horticulturist Gordon Tyrrell as director of grounds, gardens, and greenhouses. He was delighted that Tyrrell was a "keen gardener" who didn't "walk around in a starched collar." Du Pont could communicate his design ideas directly to Tyrrell, who would in turn direct the various supervisors in many simultaneous projects. Although most gardens are first planned on paper, it is likely that Harry did his design thinking while on his daily walks. Dave Richard remembers being pulled away from his job on more than one occasion to "be a tree" with arms akimbo to simulate branches. For the transplanting crew of about twenty, the method was to site plants—even trees with twenty-ton rootballs—but never actually place the soil until du Pont had had a chance to approve. As Richard reported, "He might have wanted the plant moved just a few inches this way or that."

H. F. du Pont designed intuitively, relying on what the English sculptor Henry Moore called the "haptic sense" to determine plant placement. Moore believed that a sculptor must imagine that he or she is inside the sculpture, feeling the volumes and forces pushing outward into space. As Harry walked briskly along the paths, he felt "inside" the garden. He sensed the forms in relation to one another; when he wanted a plant moved "a few inches this way or that," he was making adjustments to create an asymmetrical balance of volumes. Harry always carried a walking stick with which he may have unconsciously extended the sense of his body in space. One stick was fitted with a brass insert to hold a pencil; he frequently left tags with messages for the gardeners on a tree or shrub needing attention. When this intuitive method of designing is successful, we may be hard pressed to say exactly why we like the result. It simply feels right.

AS IF IT HAS ALWAYS BEEN THERE

In 1955 Harry and his gardeners also began developing the "good-sized area of the alfalfa field east of the Sycamore" with sweetly fragrant mock-oranges (*Philadelphus* spp.) and lilac species and hybrids. The sycamore was a venerable giant more than one hundred years old. After the Sundial Garden was completed, it was obvious to Harry that the field opposite could be used to continue the sequence of bloom into June and July. Although the specimens he chose for the huge Sycamore Area do not come into bloom one by one, there is a gentle wave of color advancing up and a little bit over the hill throughout the early summer. As the lavender of April-blooming lilacs and princess trees fades in the Sundial Garden, the soft color crosses Garden Lane and appears on the delicate littleleaf and Meyer lilacs in May and then reappears on the vigorous Preston hybrid lilacs in June (page 152). Their blooming mates are mock-oranges, *Deutzia* cultivars, American fringe trees, Oriental dogwoods, giant dogwoods, Oyama magnolias, tree lilacs, catalpas, Amur maackias, and Korean stewartias, all in white. Harry once again used one of his favorite color combinations, the pale

Overleaf left: Roses possibly carry more symbolic weight than any flower. These at Winterthur are no exception, having been planted near the end of H. F. du Pont's life, at the edge of his garden. They are unforced, natural, and perfect as only a rose in June can be. The tree blooming with white stars is Cornus kousa, the Japanese dogwood. The roses, right to left, are: 'Golden Sceptre,' yellow; 'Veilchemblou,' lavender; 'Alida Lovett,' pink; 'Purity,' white; and 'Dr. Huey,' red.

Overleaf right: H. F. du Pont had a lifelong relationship with his garden, and a stimulating dialogue with his gardeners. In the Quarry Garden, he and his men worked together to express a euphoric sense of human potential. Nothing could stop them, not even tons of rocks and small landslides. From the rock, they carved a theater-in-the-round from which to enjoy the Dionysian spectacle of "nature naturing."

lavender and vibrant red that added such verve to Azalea Woods. In June it appears on the hill in the graceful lavender fountain buddleia (*B. alternifolia*) beside an almost burgundy *Weigela* 'Eva Rathke.' He also made the unusual combination of pink and white mountain laurel underplanted with the old-fashioned rose 'Pink Leda.'

Harry conceived of the Sycamore Area as three curving paths beginning near the base of the hill and converging at the crest, which overlooks one of the most magnificent pastoral expanses at Winterthur. The primary experience for a visitor in this area is walking on the paths and admiring the individual shrubs and small flowering trees, enjoying the harmonious color scheme, and occasionally noticing vistas in other parts of the garden framed through flowers. In these pictures, distant blooms harmonize or contrast with those in the Sycamore Area and are an important element of Harry's unifying techniques.

The Sycamore Area is also beautiful from a distance. The lively assortment of shapes and sizes of trees and shrubs is reminiscent of the stage in forest succession called an old-field meadow. In June, with the hillside in bloom, the area is a romanticized old field indeed (page 153). The dense forest visible in the background, although almost a mile away, is "borrowed scenery," a design strategy used in ancient Japanese gardens to add depth and, especially if Mount Fuji could be borrowed, symbolic meaning to the garden.

The final romantic touch is a collection of old-fashioned, fragrant pink, white, lavender, and pale yellow climbing roses festooning a split-rail fence at the far end of the Sycamore Area. The fence had enclosed a barnyard for many years. In 1959 Harry decided that the animals deserved a new, sturdy fence and the roses needed the old one that looked "as if it's always been there" (page 156).

A COUNTRY PLACE

The worn fence decorated with roses symbolizes the peaceful coexistence of garden and farm. During H. F. du Pont's lifetime, the farming and dairy operations continued during Winterthur's evolution into a public institution.

By the 1950s, much of the agricultural landscape in northern New Castle County had fallen victim to urban and suburban sprawl. Harry was disheartened at the change in the surroundings and worried that "in fifty years, people won't know what a country place is like." As growth of the public Winterthur dictated revisions to the landscape, a preservationist ethos dominated his thinking.

In 1956 the Board of Trustees decided that an addition should be built onto the main museum structure to house a group of rooms that could be viewed without a reservation.

Du Pont mentioned this in a letter to James M. Scheiner, the architect who worked with Marian Coffin on the 1928–31 garden project: "We are building an addition to the Museum in that circular open space and entrance to the Museum, and I am sacrificing the rose garden and adjoining terrace for a parking space; it was either that or the meadow, and I think the meadow is more important to keep."

In the "Gardens and Grounds Notes to His Executors" of 1956, Harry said the same thing in somewhat more poetic language: "The view from the Museum entrance, down the meadow, is a charming one and must be kept permanently as a meadow, as it gives the restful, simple note which I always want Winterthur to have and which no amount of landscaping and planting can improve."

When a new visitor center and entry drive were needed in 1960, Harry planned the road with the help of some of his farmworkers. They drove across pastureland and meadows from Kennett Pike to the construction site many times until Harry was satisfied with the journey. The design is a masterpiece of understatement. For half a mile the gently curving roadway reveals an arcadian scene at each bend: groves of trees, farm ponds, and rolling hills. Until the farm ceased operations in 1969, visitors each spring also saw the heifers in pasture. All this leads to a parking lot, deliberately obscured from full view by a planting of azaleas, and the Visitor Pavilion, which is surrounded by Winterthur's famous tall trees. It's a uniquely pastoral setting for a major North American museum. Du Pont showed admirable restraint in adding plants to enhance the views along the drive, except for narcissus. Bent branches made room for 50,000 daffodil bulbs that filled the cloud-shaped beds.

H. F. du Pont's last major garden areas were Oak Hill and the Quarry Garden. The work on Oak Hill shows the eighty-year-old man at the height of his creative powers. His concerns and approach remained the same as they had been for years, but there was a sureness, deftness, and expansive self-confidence as well as a willingness to experiment usually associated with youth. Gordon Tyrrell remembered: "He was mixing colors . . . I know he did it intentionally, but they were beginning to yell. There were lavenders and mauves and reds. It wasn't offensive, but I think it was a little joke of his really. And I said, 'You can't do this.' He said, 'I'm *doing* it.' And he did it."

The layered plantings of Oak Hill—graceful scarlet, turkey, and red oaks and native persimmons; a shrub layer of tea viburnums hung with pendulous clusters of orange fruit; purple beautyberries; native azaleas; evergreen hybrid azaleas in every shade of red; fall-blooming perennials, colchicum, crocus, and sternbergia—achieve in landscape architecture something of the complexity and contradiction that Robert Venturi found in great archi-

 Above: Henry Francis du Pont holding an Iris unguicularis. *1969.*

 Right: The sign on Oak Hill looking toward the Bristol Summerhouse leaves no doubt about the designer's intentions: "Keep this view open forever. H. F. du Pont, 1962."

tecture. The planting has a richness, depth, even difficulty, that is nonetheless inviting. In autumn, beneath a darkening sky and falling leaves, branches heavy with fruit, the garden proves that "ripeness is all."

The journey ends at Harry's final garden, fashioned from an abandoned stone quarry from which many of the stones used in Winterthur's walls and bridges have been taken (page 157). There, Harry Chilcott, supervisor of the transplanting crew, and his men "during the late spring, summer, and autumn of 1961 rebuilt with great skill, stone by stone, the Primula quarry." Du Pont designed a bridge as "a series of arches." His men built a mock-up in wood at the site so they could all evaluate its appearance before actual construction. Du Pont wrote in his notes to his executors:

> I designed the Primrose Quarry Bridge with the assistance of Howard Lattomus, Leslie Potts, Gordon Tyrrell, [and] Harry Chilcott, and the view from there will always be a joy forever. I am glad that my last gardening and landscaping efforts at Winterthur are closely connected with these men who, during these many years could not have been more obliging and cooperative, and I deeply appreciate their devotion.

The Winterthur garden was becoming a joy forever to many people. In his "Garden and Grounds Notes to His Executors" for 1959, Harry wrote of Azalea Woods:

> The Kurume Grove was splendid on Sunday, May 3rd, with many kinds in full bloom and others in bud. . . . At the first downpour they will lose their pristine freshness, but it has been a wonderful display. Beginning with Saturday, May the 2nd, there have been over 1,000 visitors a day—very gratifying.

The following year, du Pont reported to the British horticulturist Patrick M. Synge: "I am still gardening as actively as ever, and as 25,000 persons come to see the gardens in the six weeks they are open to the public in the spring, and are so appreciative, I am doing more and more. Eventually the gardens will be open to the public from mid-March to mid-October." In 1961 Harry du Pont summed up his hopes of the future:

> I sincerely hope that the Museum will be a continuing source of inspiration and education for all time, and that the gardens and grounds will of themselves be a country place museum where visitors may enjoy as I have, not only the flowers, trees and shrubs, but also the sunlit meadows, shady wood paths, and the peace and great calm of a country place which has been loved and taken care of for three generations.

Harry continued to perfect the plantings and add moments of delight for visitors (page 160). He designed a small Summer Shrub Area near the Visitor Pavilion and added beds of summer-blooming lilies in dazzling colors to the Sycamore Area. His very last planting is so discreet that one must be told it wasn't done by nature, a fringe of white flowering dogwood at the woodland's edge near the golf course.

Aspiring artists are often counseled to paint, or write, what they know. Harry gardened the land he knew best. His creation gives palpable form to a great love affair with Winterthur. His message is a simple one: cultivate your garden; your soul will follow. Everything is connected.

After Henry Francis du Pont died on April 11, 1969, John A. H. Sweeney, curator emeritus, reminisced:

> The last time I saw Mr. du Pont was early January in 1969. We had an appointment to photograph him for use in the dedication book for the Crowninshield Research Building. That morning, an iris had been brought in to him and it was in a vase in the living room. After about an hour of picture taking in the Green Room, Mr. du Pont said to the photographer, "Young man, do you have any color film?" The photographer said that he had, and then Mr. du Pont said, "Come into the next room and I'll show you something you won't see many other places."

As Harry posed with the little winter-blooming *Iris unguicularis* in his hand (page 160), the young man gasped in amazement, "Why, that flower is the color of this room." "Aha," said Winterthur's head gardener, his eyes gleaming with pleasure, "that's the point."

Postscript

DEAR HARRY

In the spring of 1969, when he was in his eighty-ninth year, Henry Francis du Pont became ill. Rich in honors, this man who had entered the world at a precarious four and a half pounds, who had lived life most fully and generously, now seemed to be following the pattern of life span set by his father. Harry had been a widower for some two years now. His friend Silvia Saunders had just the right words:

Dear Harry,

I hear that you are not well, and I am sorry. I will write only a word or two, but I do wish you to know that I have enjoyed, and profited in learning, from every moment I've spent with you.

I am immeasurably glad to have been on this earth while you were; and that our paths crossed several times has been my great good fortune and my joy.

. I think you are a great great man as well as a fine companion and a generous friend.

Thank you, dear Harry, for all those moments; thank you for Chelsea in '62; thank you for your beautiful Winterthur—your gift to all of us.

May your final days on earth be happy—you who have given so much happiness to
Your ever admiring and affectionate—Silvia

THE SECOND TIME AROUND

Thomas Buchter

If I see a garden that is very beautiful, I know it is a new garden.
It may have an occasional surviving wonder—a triumphant old cedar—
from the past, but I know the intensive care is of the present.
HENRY MITCHELL, *THE ESSENTIAL EARTHMAN* 1981

All through the shrubbery, in the shrubs themselves, and in the glades
around the house, little seedlings of both shrubs and trees are
constantly springing up. These must be grubbed out, as before long they
will entirely destroy the landscaping which I have created.
H. F. DU PONT, "GARDENS AND GROUNDS NOTES TO HIS EXECUTORS" 1951

When Henry Francis du Pont died in 1969, Winterthur's garden was in prime condition—beautifully and extensively planted—as near the state of perfection as possible. Yet it quickly went into decline; there had been insufficient planning for its care following du Pont's death. For more than half a century H. F. du Pont himself had directed the garden's development and, unlike the museum proper—for which he had handed over administrative responsibility to a Board of Trustees nearly twenty years earlier—he managed both its important and routine details.

Because du Pont had carried out his garden work without the fanfare that attended changes within the museum, few on the Board of Trustees or on the administrative staff were cognizant of the effort he expended on the 60 intensively planted acres surrounding the museum. Most assumed that his death meant that plantings were finished and that during the next few years the size of the garden staff could be reduced. By the early 1970s, management of the landscape design had become a low priority, and "naturalistic," the term du Pont himself used to describe his style, came to be interpreted as "letting nature take control."

The Rhododendron maximum hybrid near the entrance to the museum was impressive in full bloom but had grown so large that it separated garden areas meant to be seen together.

Nature seized that opportunity, as it always does. Aggressive shrubs expanded; weaker ones died out. Vigorous perennials crowded out delicate ones. Trees that fell were removed but not replaced. Paths became overgrown, vegetation filled streambeds, and ivy crept up stone walls, ironwork, shrubs, and even trees. Views, vistas, color combinations, and plants arranged for succession of bloom were gradually disappearing. By the end of the 1970s, a mere decade after du Pont's death, the near obliteration of design, cohesiveness, and meaning had made the garden Winterthur's sleeping beauty.

Trustee and landscape architect Elizabeth N. du Pont recognized with alarm what was happening and set about bringing a heightened awareness to the Winterthur community that a naturalistic garden indeed required a controlling hand. Between 1982 and 1987, while a member of the Board of Trustees at Winterthur, she determinedly worked to establish a management policy that would conserve the design of the garden for posterity yet recognize elements of change inherent in all living organisms. She finally prevailed, and early in 1988 we slowly began to wake our sleeping beauty.

When I came to Winterthur as the first deputy director of the newly created Garden Department, I found a dedicated and enthusiastic staff. We reorganized responsibilities to maximize productivity and created new opportunities for professional development. We began an almost daily dialogue that continues to this day about how best to manage the national treasure in our care.

In defining Winterthur garden's unique character, we concluded that it would not be appropriate to restore the plantings to a particular moment in history. H. F. du Pont was constantly clarifying his ideas. Although it is more difficult to analyze and define a designer's approach and restore the artistic intent than to merely replace a plant list from a certain year, that is the challenge we set for ourselves.

First we had to stabilize all areas of the garden—a three-year project. This entailed removing seedlings that had emerged as a result of neglect, cleaning up brush, and bringing the scale of plantings into balance with one another and with architectural features.

Once we achieved this goal we began restoring the naturalistic design of the garden—the garden as an art form rather than a discrete collection of plants. For this we set guidelines:

1. Du Pont had designed plantings with an emphasis on color, so we would give high priority to preserving and re-creating color combinations. In this we could rely on du Pont's records, which reflected his sound horticultural knowledge, spirit of innovation, and design experimentation.

2.   We would restore as many plants and plant combinations as possible. The notes du Pont made throughout his life, documenting which combinations worked and which did not, would facilitate this project.

3.   We would continue a process that du Pont had begun in the 1960s: adding shrubs, trees, and perennials to provide summer color to augment the predominant spring and autumn displays. Our goal would be to refine plantings and plant combinations to strengthen floral, textural, fruit, and foliage displays and provide year-round interest in the garden.

4.   We would restore the connection between the museum, the garden, and the rural landscape, including reopening and enhancing views from inside the museum so visitors would have the opportunity to understand the complex interrelationships between the interior and exterior and comprehend Winterthur as a conceptual whole.

THE WORK BEGINS

A common mistake in garden management is a failure to evaluate the design objectively, a tendency to accept plants that have seeded themselves and are growing because of neglect and to work around them. It becomes all too easy to let paths remain overgrown and vistas closed off—in other words, to "manage the neglect." Although the garden was in decline when I came to Winterthur in 1988, I remember feeling that the design was so powerful that it would guide us to what needed to be done if we just took time to read the landscape. We could identify paths in the grass that were slightly raised, shrubs that were planted with distinct spacing, and groupings of bulbs or perennials of which only the foliage was apparent because too much shade or competition kept the plants from blooming.

Soon after we began serious pruning, color relationships that we never knew existed became apparent among far-flung garden areas. We realized that what we had been calling the "gardens" was in reality one garden containing a series of design experiences. Through archival research we discovered that du Pont's garden notes frequently made references to paths and walks (for example, "three new azalea paths," "the cydonia walk"), words that implied motion through a single garden. With this clue we searched for evidence in the garden and found numerous shrubs and trees organized to create paths. We campaigned to change the public's perception of the space to a garden, knowing that the word *gardens* might allow us and others to fall into the trap of seeing and developing each of the areas individually without thinking about their relationships with one another.

It became clear that there was a recurring pattern in the plantings. Du Pont had achieved a layered effect through skillful use of tree, shrub, and herbaceous components.

Overleaf: In the 1930s the sunny Glade Garden contained alpine plants. Sixty years of tree growth has made it a shady spot. Six hundred hardy orchids (Bletilla striata) restore the original color scheme and design intent, while allowing the current staff to bring their creative energy to bear on renewing the garden.

Overleaf, inset: On a clear day you can see forever, if first you have cleared brush, weeded, and fertilized. After three years of rigorous horticultural renewal, scilla and chionodoxa on the March Bank flowed throughout Azalea Woods as well. It became an ocean of blue. We did not plant a single bulb; they are all descendants of those planted about 1910. As H. F. du Pont noted, "The great pleasure of a bulb-garden is in its permanence."

This technique provided visually full plantings, offered great opportunities for creating color combinations, and increased options for succession of bloom in any given area, allowing visitors to appreciate references to the natural landscape.

REFLECTING POOL AND GLADE GARDEN

The best place to begin restoring any residential garden is at the house and along the main circulation routes into the garden. We began our work at the Reflecting Pool (formerly the swimming pool), the adjacent Glade Garden, and the lawn and paths on the east side of the museum. All were part of Marian Coffin's 1928 plan. The pathways to and from the many doorways had provided easy access to the garden. Coffin had also created design elements that were to be appreciated from specific windows of what was then the du Ponts' house. By 1988 some views through these windows were completely blocked by vegetation, and some trees were out-and-out unsightly. Looking across rooms and out windows from several inside vantage points was our first step in understanding Coffin's design as it related to the museum. The second step was looking from the garden areas to the museum. A study of Coffin's plan confirmed the important relation of house to garden.

The Italianate staircase leading up to the museum from the Reflecting Pool had become overgrown with boxwood that spilled voluptuously over the coping, severely restricting the stairs. We eventually replaced the boxwood with younger plants that will be kept in bounds by regular trimming. Removal of the old boxwood returned the staircase to its full width, allowing two or more people to ascend side by side. It also revealed the skillfully cut flagstone coping on the low walls that separated stair from garden.

The bathhouses, walls, and most of the iron and brass railings near the Reflecting Pool were overgrown with ivy, obscuring graceful architectural features. We removed ivy from walls and ironwork, making notes about what needed to be repaired as we proceeded.

If anything, the transformation of the Glade Garden was even more dramatic than that of the Reflecting Pool. This naturalistic area, also designed by Coffin in 1928, had almost become a jungle. We removed or pruned the overgrown shrubs, put down new gravel on paths, and carefully weeded between rockwork, searching for any floral survivors of the original planting. There were some! Fern-leaved corydalis had seeded itself prolifically. Originally a rock garden, the Glade Garden was now so shady that, except for the corydalis and a few others, most of the sun-loving alpine plants had died out. Rather than repeat the original plant list, we searched for shade-tolerant plants that fulfilled the intimate design intent with its yellow, white, blue, rose, and lavender color scheme (pages 168–69).

PEONY GARDEN

West of the museum lay another of Marian Coffin's designs, the Peony Garden, which was originally planted with iris (page 172). Two garden structures anchor the ends of this area: Latimeria Summerhouse and a latticework open doorway placed on axis with each other. Du Pont and Coffin intended both structures to be visible from any point along the walkway between the two. By the late 1980s, however, azaleas along one end of the path had grown so tall and dense that the design relationship was all but hidden. We rejuvenated the shrubs by taking out a third to half of the growth—as much as four feet in some cases—then fertilizing and watering to encourage new growth to come from the base. The azaleas, *Rhododendron mucronatum* 'Magnifica' and *R.* 'Coral Bells,' no longer hide the garden architecture. Shrubs that serve as a backdrop for the peonies—a collection of forsythias and the beautybush (*Kolkwitzia amabilis*)—no longer obscure the view of the museum. The restored view allows an appreciation of how well du Pont and Coffin situated the expanded house in the landscape. To some extent we broke new ground in American garden restoration with the work in the Peony Garden. Most of the shrubs were fifty years old, and it was not at all certain they could tolerate such severe pruning. All did survive, and two years later, much to our delight, they bloomed as they hadn't for many years.

MARCH BANK

The March Bank, just north of the museum conservatory, is an area devoted primarily to winter- and spring-blooming bulbs, but *Hosta ventricosa*, white snakeroot, tawny daylily, roving bellflower, and the fruit display of double-file viburnum do provide summer color. Stabilization began with summer weeding. Horticulturists moved as a team among the viburnums and ground cover plantings of hosta, vinca, euonymus, and pachysandra, cutting down weeds. The viburnums had become so large that they grew together; we reduced their height by two-thirds, allowing the ground covers and bulbs to grow back into areas that had been shaded. In the autumn we used mulching mowers to chop up the fallen leaves and plant debris and then applied fertilizer.

The chionodoxa and scilla, which had been reduced to "pools of blue" for many years, were transformed the following spring into "oceans of color" that could be viewed from walkways through the area and, because of extensive pruning and clearing, from more distant vantage points throughout the garden.

Below the March Bank the small stream had gradually filled with viburnum and rose seedlings. After cutting these down, we pulled out the invaders' root systems. A wonderful

combination of late white daffodils and Virginia bluebells revealed themselves the following spring. They had been there many years, overpowered by the invading vegetation.

As work continued and design elements became more evident in this area, we pondered over a path that had become completely overgrown. Only after using it one day did we recognize that it gave greater coherence to the area and offered a panoramic view of the conservatory, March Bank, and Azalea Woods from different points along its length.

AZALEA WOODS

Azalea Woods, perhaps the best-known planting at Winterthur, had survived virtually intact, although several fierce storms in the 1970s and 1980s had taken out part of the canopy. Plants had become so tall, however, that they obscured the magnificent color combinations and their relationship to the interplanted wildflowers and dogwood. Only the broadest design details were evident. A major pruning brought plants below eye level so that color harmonies were readily seen. By pruning groups of Kurume azaleas at various heights, we created a natural-looking, undulating display. Torch azaleas (R. kaempferi) that du Pont used to create a corridor effect at one of the paths into Azalea Woods were left fairly tall but were opened up so that new growth came from the base for better flower distribution throughout the plant, producing as much color as possible. All plants were trimmed back from paths to allow visitors comfortable access. By the time we finished pruning, we had taken out sixty truckloads of azalea trimmings. We completed the stabilization with fertilizer and water.

THE PINETUM

The Pinetum planting initiated by Henry Algernon du Pont in 1918 was transformed by his son into an evergreen background for flowering trees, shrubs, and perennials. As H. F. du Pont explained to Marian Coffin in 1939, "I am also adding more plants to my Cydonia [flowering quince] walk, as I think that it is one of the most beautiful features of the place."

At one end of the Pinetum is a partially walled viewing area called the Blue Atlas Cedar Circle. By the late 1980s the space was filled with the graceful but low-hanging branches of the cedar. After considerable thought, discussion, and review of our commitment to restoring design elements, we recognized that it was important to reestablish the garden space and once again put furniture in the circle, providing a place for people to gather and look out toward the Sundial Garden to the south and east. To open up the view we needed to remove branches from the blue atlas cedar and prune and thin out other plants

The Peony Garden is located halfway along a path from the Visitor Pavilion to the museum. In late May and early June the Saunders hybrid tree peonies are in full bloom; their flowers somehow manage to be both voluptuous and delicate at the same time.

173

such as the Sargent crabapples. The restored view includes nearby displays in the Sundial Garden area and great sweeps of bulbs in the distance, one of du Pont's recurrent design techniques to unify the garden.

Prunus 'Accolade' is a lovely cherry and said to be du Pont's favorite at Winterthur. We had looked at a specimen growing near the blue atlas cedar and thought that it was a bit too crowded and needed to come out. Revisiting the area in the spring we recognized that the cherry was a beacon of light drawing people from other areas of the garden. It was part of a very dramatic display of delicate pink flowering trees and shrubs surrounded by dark green conifers. We left it.

SUNDIAL GARDEN

The April-blooming Sundial Garden replaced the tennis and croquet courts in 1955; by the late 1980s this area, too, had become overgrown. Lilacs were ten to fifteen feet tall and had flowers only at the top, which prevented visitors from noticing the exquisite color combinations. Quince, spireas, and early rhododendrons were also too tall and too thick. We gave them all a heavy pruning to reduce their height and thin out the stems. Only then was the human scale of this "garden room" reestablished.

The plantings presented other problems. The boxwood hedge around the sundial was in serious decline even though it was the third time it had been replaced. The heavy soil, which had to be broken up by air hammers in 1955, was once again proving inhospitable. Our only choice was to remove the boxwood and begin the search for a fine-textured, evergreen replacement from a different genus that would maintain design intent. Curators and horticulturists on the Sundial Garden restoration team are still evaluating their options.

QUARRY GARDEN

The Quarry Garden was the last major landscaping effort at Winterthur by H. F. du Pont. As an exhausted quarry, the area sat for many years before du Pont decided to use it as a site for growing primroses.

By the late 1980s the area was completely overgrown. Grasses and *Primula japonica* had crowded out the more delicate primulas, except for a few plants of *P.* x *bullesiana*; rockwork had become covered with ivy; shrubs and trees dominated planting spaces in the rocks; woodchucks had burrowed between rocks, creating enormous erosion problems; and stepping stones were partially silted over. Removing the ivy and many "volunteer" shrubs was the first step in the year-long general cleanup. Pruning trees that surrounded the area opened views and let in air and light. We reestablished planting pockets in the walls, completed the stone path along the west side, made two small waterfalls by creating rills for spring water to flow down the rock face, and, using small stones, relined the beds of the three streams that flow out of the quarry floor. Having removed all plants from the bog at the bottom, we brought in leaf mold and rototilled to create optimum growing conditions for the herbaceous plants to be introduced. New plantings include 1,600 *Primula* x *bullesiana* and smaller quantities of 9 other rare primulas that restore du Pont's color scheme and plant list. *Lobelia cardinalis*, *L. siphilitica*, ligularias, anemones, chelones, and other perennials are new additions that will provide bloom throughout the summer.

BRISTOL SUMMERHOUSE

Bristol Summerhouse, installed at the top of the hill immediately east of the Quarry Garden in the 1960s, offers a beautiful panorama of the lower ponds, the Winterthur train station, the intervening pastureland, and hillside woodlands, making it an ideal spot for visitors to enjoy the rural landscape (page 176). We wanted to refine the landscape and maintain the pastoral setting, not turn it into a garden. We now cut the fields for hay in June and October. Between mowings, grasses grow tall and sway in the breeze. The fields are scattered with wildflowers; birds and small animals find abundant food and cover. We agree with du Pont's comment that "no amount of landscaping can improve it."

The approach to Bristol Summerhouse is from the north, along a planting of June-blooming trees and shrubs known as the Sycamore Area. These "woodies" had been supplemented with herbaceous plants—largely lilies and other summer-blooming varieties that have died out. Our plan is to restore that herbaceous layer, redefine the paths, and replace shrubs that have been removed. The eastern edge of this area has a post-and-rail fence planted with old-fashioned climbing roses, including 'Dr. W. Van Fleet,' and marks the transition from garden to rural landscape. We replaced some roses that had died with a "sport," or natural mutation of 'Dr. W. Van Fleet' called 'New Dawn,' which has the same form and fragrance as its parent but blooms throughout the summer.

RESTORATION: ADDING COLOR

The decision to set aside a three-year cleanup period before beginning any major replanting proved to be a propitious one. We needed time to bring order to the garden, raise the level of maintenance, and address myriad managerial, curatorial, and educational issues. The three-year "breathing space" gave us an opportunity to determine which plants had been

lost or crowded out and to establish a plan for building on the summer-flowering displays that du Pont had begun to work out in the 1960s.

Where are we now? A generous gift enabled us to restore the beautifully coordinated detail of the Winterhazel Walk. The Quarry Garden is redone in du Pont's exhilarating color scheme of mauve, rose, lavender, pink, ochre, yellow, peach, and tangerine. A mass planting of pink roses has been restored to Magnolia Bend. Spring- and summer-blooming trees, shrubs, and herbaceous plants installed in an area south of the Reflecting Pool have brought lavender, pink, and white to the summer garden. A massive project along the stream by the front entrance drive to the estate has involved volunteers who replanted tens of thousands of *Primula japonica*. Work is scheduled for Oak Hill and the Sycamore Area, as are further refinements to Azalea Woods and the Sundial Garden.

Stabilizing and restoring the garden is exponential in effect. There is more abundant flowering; the pruning and clearing have allowed each area to be seen from multiple vantage points near and far, oblique and tangential. Visitors have always liked the garden. Now they revel in it.

In the future, we expect to use plants in creative and innovative ways, just as H. F. du Pont did. The garden is organic, ever-developing; the future is just as important as the past. As we preserve and build on du Pont's design intent, we will also follow his lead in continuing to try new ideas and rework plantings so they become better every year.

The documentation of successful additions to the landscape, which du Pont started some ninety years ago, will continue to play an important role. We will remove plantings that do not work, as he did quite diligently. Like Henry Francis du Pont, we do not plan to "live with" our mistakes. We will consider them part of a learning process as we correct and perfect the space.

The future holds great promise for the Winterthur garden, an extraordinary example of the important movement in American landscape design that took place in the first half of the twentieth century. It will always be not only a truly great American garden but a tribute to the art and craft of gardening itself.

Bristol Summerhouse with fallen tulip-poplar leaves.

BIBLIOGRAPHY

Primary sources for "Nurturing a Family Tradition" were the Longwood and Winterthur manuscript collections at Hagley Museum and Library (Wilmington, Delaware), the premier repository for du Pont papers and company records. Certain unpublished studies were also helpful on specific subjects: Roy Boatman, "The Agricultural Establishment at Eleutherian Mills, 1802–1834" (Hagley Research Report, 1961); and Elizabeth P. McLean, "The Horticultural Heritage of the Brandywine Valley" (paper delivered at the Brandywine Valley Gardens conference, Winterthur, 1988), which discusses the Quaker horticultural influence in Philadelphia.

Valencia Libby's "Henry Francis du Pont and the Early Development of Winterthur Gardens, 1880–1927" (Master's thesis, University of Delaware, 1984) was an important source for several authors. Winterthur Archives at Winterthur Library also proved to be an invaluable source for much of the information throughout the book, particularly the personal correspondence of H. F. du Pont.

Brookes, John. *Room Outside*. New York: Penguin Books, 1979.

Browning, Ted. *Notes from Turtle Creek*. Chadds Ford, Pa.: Brandywine Conservancy, 1991.

Bruce, Harold. *How to Grow Wildflowers and Wild Shrubs and Trees in Your Own Garden*. New York: Alfred A. Knopf, 1976.

———. *Winterthur in Bloom*. Winterthur, Del.: Henry Francis du Pont Winterthur Museum, 1986.

Cantor, Jay E. *Winterthur*. New York: Harry N. Abrams, 1985.

Chinard, Gilbert. *The Correspondence of Jefferson and du Pont de Nemours*. Baltimore: Johns Hopkins University Press, 1931.

Crowe, Sylvia. *Garden Design*. New York: Hearthside Press, 1959.

Fleming, E. McClung. "The History of the Winterthur Estate." In *Winterthur Portfolio One*, edited by Milo M. Naeve, pp. 9–51. Winterthur, Del.: Henry Francis du Pont Winterthur Museum, 1964.

Hiss, Anthony. *The Experience of Place*. New York: Alfred A. Knopf, 1990.

Jackson, J. B. *American Space: The Centennial Years, 1865–1879*. New York: W. W. Norton, 1972.

———. *Landscapes*. Edited by Ervin H. Zube. Amherst: University of Massachusetts Press, 1970.

———. *The Necessity for Ruins*. Amherst: University of Massachusetts Press, 1980.

Jefferson, Thomas. *Observations sur la Virginie.* Paris: Chez Barrois, 1786.

Jekyll, Gertrude. *Wood and Garden: Notes and Thoughts, Practical and Critical, of a Working Amateur.* 1914. Reprint. Salem, N.H.: Ayer Co., 1983.

———. *Colour Schemes for the Flower Garden.* 1914. Reprint. Salem, N.H.: Ayer Co., 1983.

Kasson, John F. *Civilizing the Machine: Technology and Republican Values in America, 1776–1900.* New York: Grossman Publishers, 1976.

La Rochefoucauld-Liancourt, François. *Voyage dans les Etats-Unis d'Amérique fait en 1795, 1796, et 1797.* Paris: Chez du Pont Imprimerie-Libraire, 1799.

Munroe, John A. "The Philadelawareans: A Study in the Relations between Philadelphia and Delaware in the Late Eighteenth Century." *Pennsylvania Magazine of History and Biography* 69, no. 2 (April 1945): 128–49.

Pursell, Carroll W., Jr. "E. I. du Pont and the Merino Mania in Delaware, 1805–1815." *Agricultural History* 36, no. 2 (April 1962): 91–100.

Robinson, William. *The English Flower Garden.* 1883. Reprint. New York: Amaryllis Press, 1984.

Rybczynski, Witold. *Looking Around: A Journey through Architecture.* New York: Viking, 1992.

———. *Waiting for the Weekend.* New York: Viking, 1991.

Saricks, Ambrose. *Pierre Samuel du Pont de Nemours.* Lawrence: University of Kansas Press, 1965.

Scott, Jane. *Botany in the Field: An Introduction to Plant Communities for the Amateur Naturalist.* Englewood Cliffs, N.J.: Prentice-Hall, 1984.

Scott-James, Anne. *Sissinghurst.* London: Michael Joseph, 1974.

Spongberg, Stephen A. *A Reunion of Trees: The Discovery of Exotic Plants and Their Introduction into North American and European Landscapes.* Cambridge: Harvard University Press, 1990.

Stevens, Wallace. *Collected Poems.* New York: Alfred A. Knopf, 1954.

Sweeney, John A. H. *Henry Francis du Pont, 1880–1969.* Winterthur, Del.: Henry Francis du Pont Winterthur Museum, 1986.

Thacker, Christopher. *The History of Gardens.* Berkeley and Los Angeles: University of California Press, 1979.

Tyrrell, C. Gordon. "The History and Development of the Winterthur Gardens." In *Winterthur Portfolio One,* edited by Milo M. Naeve, pp. 122–38. Winterthur, Del.: Henry Francis du Pont Winterthur Museum, 1964.

Weidensaul, Scott. *Seasonal Guide to the Natural Year.* Golden, Colo.: Fulcrum Publishing, 1992.

CHRONOLOGY

1800	Pierre Samuel du Pont de Nemours, sons Victor Marie and Eleuthère Irénée and their families arrive in America.
1802	E. I. du Pont establishes gunpowder manufactory, E. I. du Pont de Nemours & Co.
1810–18	E. I. du Pont purchases four tracts of land forming the nucleus of what later becomes Winterthur.
1837	Jacques Antoine and Evelina du Pont Bidermann purchase the property and name their home-to-be Winterthur.
1867	Henry du Pont purchases Winterthur.
1876	Henry Algernon and Mary Pauline Foster du Pont settle at Winterthur.
c. 1880	*Magnolia* x *soulangiana* planted at "the bend" (Magnolia Bend) by Henry A. du Pont.
1880	Henry Francis (H. F.) du Pont is born.
1899	Enters Harvard.
1901	Begins taking courses at Bussey Institution; goes on first trip abroad.
1902	Mary Pauline Foster du Pont dies; H. F. du Pont plants Narcissus Grove.
1903	Graduates from Harvard; begins to manage household for his father; undertakes extensive work in the greenhouses.
1906	Henry Algernon du Pont elected to U. S. Senate; H. F. du Pont begins to manage Washington home as well as Winterthur.
1909	H. F. du Pont takes over supervision of the Winterthur gardens and grounds; visits gardens in Europe with Marian Coffin and her mother; begins planting "bank to bend" (the March Bank).
1910–16	Has autochromes taken of garden.
1912	Travels in Europe from May to September; attends the Royal International Horticultural Exhibition and visits many gardens, including Gertrude Jekyll's, William Robinson's, and Ellen Willmott's; again traveling with Marian Coffin and her mother.
1914	Becomes manager of Winterthur Farms.
1916	Marries Ruth Wales.

1917	Purchases Kurume azaleas from Cottage Gardens Co.
1918	Charles Sprague Sargent suggests planting of a pinetum at Winterthur.
1923	Winterhazel Walk begun.
1926	House in Southampton completed (Chestertown House); Marian Coffin landscapes grounds; Henry Algernon du Pont dies.
1928	Major addition to Winterthur house begun; H. F. du Pont asks Marian Coffin to create landscape design for the environs of the building and several outlying areas.
1929	Swimming pool, Glade Garden, and Iris Garden begun.
c. 1938	Quince Walk established.
1946	Saunders Peony Garden planted.
1950s	Planting in Sycamore Area begun; plantings on Oak Hill augmented.
1951	Museum is opened to public.
1955	Marian Coffin draws plan for April Garden (Sundial Garden); 18,000 daffodils planted on golf course and in Sycamore Area.
1956	H. F. du Pont receives Medal of Honor from the Garden Club of America; South Wing added to museum.
1957	Marian Coffin dies.
1959	Native azaleas planted on Oak Hill.
1959–60	Visitor Pavilion, parking area, front drive, upper ponds created.
1961	Quarry Garden started.
1964–65	Lower ponds created.
1967	Ruth Wales du Pont dies.
1969	H. F. du Pont dies on April 11.
1986	Special task force to study Winterthur's garden and grounds appointed by the chairman of the Board of Trustees.
1988	Thomas Buchter appointed deputy director, Garden Department; three-year plan for garden stabilization begun.
1989	Special gifts given for restoration of Winterhazel Walk and Quarry Garden.
1991	Renewal of Reflecting Pool and Glade Garden.
1993	Special gifts given for restoration of Sundial Garden.

GENEALOGY

Pierre Samuel du Pont de Nemours
(1739–1817)
Publisher & economist living in France
m. 1766 Nicole Charlotte Marie Louise le Dée de Rencourt
(1743–1787)
2 children

Eleuthère Irénée du Pont
(1771–1834)
Founder of E.I. du Pont de Nemours & Co.
m. 1791 Sophie Madeleine Dalmas
(1775–1828)
7 children*

Evelina Gabrielle du Pont
(1796–1863)
m. 1816 Jacques Antoine Bidermann
(1790–1865)
Partner, E.I. du Pont de Nemours & Co.
1 child

James Irénée Bidermann
(1817–1890)
Engineer
m. 1844 Gabrielle Camille Bégue
5 children

Gen. Henry du Pont
(1812–1889)
Partner, E.I. du Pont de Nemours & Co.
& gentleman farmer
m. 1837 Louisa Gerhard
(1816–1900)
8 children*

Col. Henry Algernon du Pont
(1838–1926)
Gentleman farmer & U.S. Senator
m. 1874 Mary Pauline Foster
(1849–1902)
2 children*

Henry Francis du Pont
(1880–1969)
Gentleman farmer & collector
m. 1916 Ruth Wales
(1891–1967)
2 children

Pauline Louise (du Pont) Harrison
(b. 1918)

Ruth Ellen (du Pont) Lord
(b. 1922)

* surviving to adulthood

AUTHOR'S ACKNOWLEDGMENTS

Almost fifteen years ago, members of the Garden Club of Wilmington began a project of sorting through thousands of letters, diaries, plant lists, seed orders and catalogues, and annotated articles from horticulture magazines in the Winterthur Archives. After several years of digging, the volunteers had unearthed the raw data of what they realized was a fascinating chapter of American garden history. The late Elizabeth N. du Pont, a member of both the garden club and the Winterthur Board of Trustees, urged Valencia Libby, then a graduate student in the Longwood Program in Ornamental Horticulture, to consider writing her master's thesis on Winterthur. The result appeared in June 1984, as "Henry Francis du Pont and the Early Development of Winterthur Gardens, 1880–1927." We all owe an enormous debt of gratitude to these pioneering researchers.

In 1988, less than a month after Thomas Buchter became the first deputy director of the newly formed Garden Department, I approached him with a proposal for a book that would tell the Winterthur garden story to a wider audience, to be written by several authors including himself. Much to his credit and my delight, he enthusiastically accepted the idea and enlisted the crucial support of Thomas A. Graves, Jr., then the director of Winterthur. This book owes its existence to them as much as anyone.

Many colleagues at Winterthur have helped me in countless ways since then. A few who deserve special thanks are: Charles F. Hummel and the Research Committee; John A. H. Sweeney; Eleanor McD. Thompson and Heather H. Clewell of the Library Division; Karol A. Schmiegel, Grace Eleazer, and photographers Herbert L. Crossan III, George J. Fistrovich, and Wayne Gibson of the Registration Division; Ruth Bryant Power of the Information Systems Division; Linda R. Eirhart, Nancy Kubnick (creator of the watercolor garden map), D. Leslie Ferst, and Janet Elling (who kept the trams running on time) in the Landscape Division; John Feliciani and the Horticulture Division for waking our "sleeping beauty" of a garden; Catherine E. Hutchins, director of the Publications Division, for her skillful early editing of the manuscript; Teresa A. Vivolo, who copyedited the book; and my deepest gratitude to the unflappable Onie Rollins, my editor at Winterthur. Linda L. Barry of the Garden Department not only typed and retyped the manuscript but also had numerous valuable suggestions and made me laugh when things seemed grim.

Early in the writing I had fruitful conversations with Carol E. Hoffecker, David Schuyler, Averell du Pont, and Warren Hunting Smith, a friend of Marian Coffin. George Colman, H. F. du Pont's "right hand man" for many years, shared wonderful memories and insights. David S. Richard recounted his memories of H. F. du Pont's working methods in the garden. Howard Lattomus spoke about the farming operations with Paul Hensley. Carol Ann Long and Brian Cox provided information on Ruth du Pont's music education.

Thomas Buchter and I are grateful for the encouragement we received from the Garden Committee, most ably chaired by Dolly Fisher, and from Pauline L. Harrison and Ruth E. Lord, daughters of Henry Francis and Ruth Wales du Pont. I have thanked "my authors" many times, and do so here, as well as Carol Betsch, who captured just the right feeling in her extraordinary photographs. It was a joyful experience to work with her. I was happy to be able to use some of Gottlieb Hampfler's superb photographs and the room studies taken by Lizzie Himmel for *Winterthur* by Jay E. Cantor (Abrams, 1985).

A. Lorraine Lanmon; Judith B. Tankard; James M. Smith, director emeritus of Winterthur; and Carol Betsch helped me greatly by reading and commenting on the manuscript. Dwight P. Lanmon, the present director of Winterthur, kindly saw the project to completion. At Abrams the astute Mark D. Greenberg, the project manager; Jennifer Stockman, editor; and Maria L. Miller, the designer, transformed our work into a beautiful reality.

On a personal note, I would like to mention two former teachers, both now deceased but alive in my memories. Armistead (Ted) Browning taught me that a garden can be expressive of our deepest feelings for nature. Harold (Hal) Bruce helped me see that the Winterthur garden is a shining example of a garden as art.

I thank my family for their enthusiasm throughout what must have seemed like an endless process, especially my parents, Eugene J. and Edythe Magnani, and my son, Matthew Schweizer. And finally, I give thanks to a couple who worked as a team, although they never met. My former husband, Edward Schweizer, in numerous discussions challenged, prodded, analyzed, soothed, and pushed me to keep going, and Ruth N. Joyce, my research associate and friend, caught me when I fell. I could not, would not, have done it without them.

PHOTOGRAPHER'S ACKNOWLEDGMENTS

With gratitude, I thank Valencia Libby for initially suggesting that I turn my photographer's eye from the landscape toward the garden and for introducing me to Winterthur, where H. F. du Pont has combined them with such inspired vision. My heartfelt thanks to friends in the Garden Department—Linda Barry, Thomas Buchter, Linda Eirhart, Janet Elling, John Feliciani, Ruth Joyce, and Denise Magnani—for welcoming me home each time I visited. Special mention is due Robert Buckley and his staff at Buckley Photo Lab in Wilmington. Their rare combination of high professional standards, consummate service, and graciousness made the technical aspect of this project not only possible but pleasurable.

INDEX

PHOTOGRAPH CREDITS

All photographs are by Carol Betsch except those that appear on the pages listed here. Courtesy Cornell Capa, Magnum Photos: 138. Courtesy Hagley Museum and Library, Wilmington, Delaware: 52, 53, 66 above left and right. Courtesy Winterthur: 132 (George Fistrovich); 119, 121, 125 inset, 126 (Wayne Gibson); 108, 114 right (Samuel Gottscho); 6 inset, 18, 22, 23, 81, 88, 125 (Gottlieb Hampfler); 114 left, 115 inset, 118 center and right inset, 124 inset (Lizzie Himmel); 118 left inset, 176 (Robert C. Lautman); 80, 89 (H. B. McCollum); 58, 62, 66 below, 72, 73, 90, 111, 112, 113, 131, 160 left (photographer unknown)

Additional Credits: Courtesy Hagley Museum and Library, Wilmington, Delaware: 40, 41, 45, 46, 47, 48, 49, 50, 54, 55, 56, 57, 59, 60. Courtesy Winterthur: 20, 69, 79, 110